Ciao, Battista

CIAO, BATTISTA

memoirs of my life

BATTISTA ANTONIO LOCATELLI

CHAPEL HILL
PRESS

Copyright © 2015 Battista Antonio Locatelli

All rights reserved. No part of this book may be used, reproduced
or transmitted in any form or by any means, electronic or mechanical,
including photograph, recording, or any information storage or
retrieval system, without the express written permission
of the author, except where permitted by law.

ISBN 978-1-59715-107-8
Library of Congress Catalog Number 2014959918

Second Printing

To my loving wife for her support and help through all these years. I couldn't have done it without you. I love you, Rio.

On our wedding day

Contents

Foreword ix

Preface and Acknowledgments xi

Chapter One: The Bull of Santa Cruz, 1877–1907 1

Chapter Two: My Father Grows Up, 1908–1930 5

Chapter Three: My Early Life in Italy, 1931–1945 7

Chapter Four: The Second World War, 1939–1945 15

Chapter Five: Switzerland, 1945–1949 23

Chapter Six: America, 1949–1952 31

Chapter Seven: Married with Children, 1952–1955 39

Chapter Eight: Hollywood, 1955–1962 43

Chapter Nine: A Singing Career? 1962–1969 53

Chapter Ten: A Restaurant Is Born, 1969–1979 63

Chapter Eleven: Seeing Stars 83

Chapter Twelve: New Experiences, 1980–2000 95

Chapter Thirteen: The End of an Era 103

Afterword: Ciao, Present 107

Foreword

This book has been a long time coming—longer than I've been alive. It has been a long-standing desire of our family for my grandfather, Battista Locatelli, to record his stories and experiences. It especially means a lot to me to have these memories preserved to share with my own children. So thank you, Grandpa, for taking the time to make this book. It has been an unforgettable, special experience learning about and from you.

This has been a group effort with a great deal of help from my mother, Heidi; my aunts Pier and Desiree; my uncle Gigli; my great aunts—especially Irene, Marcella, and Tina; and of course, the backbone of our family, my dearly loved Mamacita Rio, without whom this book would not have been the same.

Each person—especially the brothers and sisters—who has lived alongside Battista at any point in his life will have a unique interpretation, recollection, or details and facts that could vary or enhance my grandfather's book. We hope we do not give any offense in these memoirs as we've endeavored to record everything as accurately as possible and as faithfully as recalled. Here is his story, in his words (with minor changes for clarity).

Gretchen Smith
Granddaughter of Battista Locatelli

Preface and Acknowledgments

Hello. My name is Battista Antonio Locatelli. I was born 12/10/31 in a little town, Berbenno. The closest city to it is Bergamo. It is just north of Milan.

Today I live in a small town in the state of Utah in the great country of America, and I have had a full life. I have four children whom I love and am proud of. I have eleven grandchildren and, as of 2014, I have nine great-grandchildren. I have been blessed.

And I have been blessed and so lucky to have the opportunity to meet and talk one-to-one with the people, the builders of Las Vegas. Lou Weiner, Larry Ruvo, mayors Carolyn and Oscar Goodman. The sheriffs of Las Vegas: Ralph Lamb, John Moran, and Jerry Keller. There are more people: Hank Greenspun, the owner of the newspaper the *Las Vegas Sun* and the builder and founder of Green Valley, Nevada. Moe Dalitz, Cecil Lynch, Major Riddle, Michael Gaughan, Horst Dziura, and of course Mr. Las Vegas, Steve Wynn, followed by Kirk Kerkorian. In my own small way, I'm glad to have contributed and been there for the growth of Las Vegas, but I also want to thank these people; they enjoyed me as a person of interest, and that humbles me. I am honored to have our lives touch.

Our very dear friends Dean and Gerda Koontz have been an inspiration to us over the years, and we are so thankful for their wonderful friendship.

Battista's Hole in the Wall was a great love and family affair that still continues on without me. I had so much help from my children and their spouses and friends, my grandchildren, my brother Vittorio and sisters Marcella and Irene, and my nieces and nephews. Without them it could not have been the success it continues to be today.

But of course, everything I have accomplished I would not have been able to do without my wife, Rio. Despite our different personalities, she did everything. Never, never, never complained. I love you, Rio.

Chapter One

The Bull of Santa Cruz

1877–1907

My grandfather, Pietro "Pete" Locatelli, was born in Italy on June 18, 1877. He immigrated to America in August of 1895 with his brother Giuseppe. He chose to settle in Santa Cruz, California, because other Locatellis had immigrated there. Not direct relatives, but perhaps from another branch of the family.

They went up the valley, Felton Valley, very well known in Boulder Creek. And as I understand it, he went into the woodcutting business because, back in Italy, our family knew a lot about cutting trees. They settled in one of the tallest and densest forests of beautiful redwood trees. Of course, he didn't have any electric cutting machine back then. They would use a large crosscut saw; it was about eight to ten feet long with two big handles. And of course these men that did the sawing, they were built out of real muscle, not hamburger. These redwoods, they were so big you could drive a car through some.

So when he was about twenty-two he decided to marry a young lady, Maria Teresa Salvi, from Italy. She came to America at age eighteen, in March 1902. She married my grandfather, and they had two children. Of course, they were living in a little cabin in the woods, no toilets or running water, with a dirt floor—cold, very cold. They had been a hundred times better off in Italy. At least over there they had houses; they had toilets. In Italy, living conditions were at least a hundred years ahead of Boulder Creek and the forest like this with the wild animals, bears and mountain lions and such. Anyway, it was a nightmare for her.

There was no midwife nearby. My grandfather watched the delivery of the first baby, and then he was to help with the next babies that came along. When it came time to deliver the third baby, there were complications of some kind during childbirth, and Teresa died along with the child, whom they named Fiorindo.

After Teresa died, my grandfather was going to be forced to put the children in an orphanage, but Teresa's sister, Santina Caterina Salvi, said she would come to America. So my grandfather went back to Italy to marry her, and they arrived back in America on November twentieth, 1905. Shortly after that, she was pregnant, and on April 18, 1906, the earthquake came to San Francisco—early, early in the morning. It was a horrible disaster, and it even shook Santa Cruz and the mountains and forest where my grandfather and grandmother were living. You can imagine my grandmother, Caterina, was really panicking, being pregnant in a strange country in the mountains and one of the worst earthquakes of all time hits. Boy. Anyway, she bore my dad Battista on November 3, 1906. Now Caterina had only been twenty-one when she came to America, so she was homesick and life was very hard in the mountains, so when she got pregnant again a year or so later, my grandparents decided that they would go back to Italy. Caterina made the long journey to Italy, pregnant, with the three boys all alone.

Meanwhile, my grandfather Pete was supposed to sell the property in California and the little bit of things he had and would join them in Italy within a couple years, but that time never came. He never went back to Italy, never, never, never. As I understood it, he never sent any money or anything and his youngest son, Guiseppe, who was born in Italy in June 1908, grew up never seeing his father once. So Caterina raised the four boys—Oreste; Adolfo; my father, Battista; and the youngest, Guiseppe, whom we called Bepo—by herself over there in Italy. She had family there to help I'm sure, her brothers and sisters to help with raising the boys. Caterina got work washing clothes in the public village fountain for other people, maybe cleaning house, sewing, ironing, helping out. What she did exactly, I don't know for sure.

Caterina with her four boys

Chapter Two

My Father Grows Up
1908–1930

My father growing up, he was pretty sick as a young kid. All of the boys were because nutrition was pretty bad and because they had to go out and work by the time they were four, five, six years old doing little somethings, anything they could do: picking up rocks, helping their momma in the garden, picking corn, cutting weeds, cutting hay, hauling the hay. They would carry manure down to the field in these little woven baskets with straps over their shoulders. They worked really hard. Of course, I had to do a lot of that myself when I was growing up, starting at four, five, six. You know, this is almost a joke, but one of the things in those days was that when we were born, we no sooner came out of the womb, we were given a pick and shovel to go out and start working. It is a little bit of a joke, but close to the truth. There were cows to milk, goats, chickens to feed, feed the pigs, feed the cows, stables to clean. A lot of work. A lot of work.

And my dad, he was a real go-getter type of person at a very young age. He would earn a penny and stretch that penny into a dollar and take that dollar and stretch it into a hundred dollars. I really don't know exactly the age, but at twelve, thirteen, fourteen he bought a couple donkeys, and he started to haul wood and hay and other things for people. Then he got a little wagon towing things, a couple of horses, and by the time he was eighteen, nineteen, twenty he was a little entrepreneur already.

Then he met Angelina, my momma. She was born June 28, 1908. So they both would have been in their early twenties when they got married in December of 1929. My momma was the most loving Angelina ever. Her name was Angela, but she was called Angelina because she was very petite. Most beautiful with blonde hair and blue eyes and a gorgeous singing voice. Maybe this is where I got my love of music and ability to sing. She gave so much love. Her last name was also Locatelli, prior to marrying my dad. They were not related; Locatelli is a large family name up north in Italy. In fact, we have a little town and it's called Locatello, and that is where the name came from, and our crest is an owl.

Sometime after they got married, my father bought a little, tiny truck, an old clunker. It had rubber tire wheels, not inflated. It reminded me of an old Model T Ford except a little bit longer so we could carry some things like dry leaves for people's gardens in the city. It was a little putt-putt, not even a seatbelt in it—in those days seatbelts hadn't even been invented yet—and of course he expected me to learn to drive it overnight, and I did. I drove the dang thing right off the start. Once I remember driving on a very narrow gravel road with nothing but potholes and rocks. I hit a rock with the front wheel of the truck and Dad hit me. It didn't do any damage to the tires since they were hard rubber—but I did get in trouble.

My dad always had a little something going for him. His nickname was Rescia—risk-taker, somebody who takes chances. It was even put on his tombstone after he died, November 3, 1997. But he was a real provider. He managed a nickel.

Chapter Three

My Early Life in Italy
1931–1945

My mother had several of us children to where we were all born within a year of each other. The church forbade the use of birth control, and so my older sister Giannina was born in January 1931, just one year after my parents were married, and I was born December of the same year. When I was born, I was weak. We were born too close together. Mom and Dad had a total of thirteen children. I don't know if there were any miscarriages or anything. I remember there was a little sister who died at around six months old, maybe younger than that. Her name was Ornella. When the next child came, a girl, they named her Ornella.

We had a little property with a barn on it, a couple of cows, goats, pigs, a half a dozen sheep or more, and this and that. We had a little orchard and of course we raised some corn, wheat, mainly enough to feed our growing family and a few neighbors. We had to cut all of that, and we had to peel it ourselves with a special spatula to get the corn out. We took it to a special mill, run by water or donkey, to have it ground for us. The country was moving ahead but still very immature in many ways.

My dad had his brother Oreste working for him for a few years; my cousin Fiorindo, he worked for us. My dad had me working anywhere from seven to fifteen hours a day: milking the cow, doing this, go do that. Work, work,

My parents with all of us children, minus Silvia. I am third from the left, the tallest boy.

work, and more work, and if there was no work, he would find something to keep this boy busy.

My dad had the first phone in that town—to where when we were little kids we'd be getting a phone call from somebody to deliver a message in the middle of the night. He would get one of us up. Most of the time it was me because I was the eldest son (but still a really young kid), and we'd walk maybe one hour, two hours somewhere, someplace to deliver the phone message. It didn't matter if it was cold, rainy, or sunny. I remember sometimes I was so scared at night. It was a religious and superstitious time. I'd hear some strange sound or creaking noise and think it was a ghost, and then I'd run like a ripped monkey.

I was raised in a time when punishment—spankings or beatings—were normal. Parents did not have time to baby their babies. You had to grow up real quick. My dad, having had a very tough upbringing himself, was a very tough father. I had to do a lot of fast growing up because my dad was very demanding, and he would only tell you something one time, and you'd either do it or if you didn't do it right, there would be some consequence to be paid. This helped make me the man I am today. I learned so much through work having had so little. I really learned how to survive, to make things happen. I don't blame him for how he treated us. He had no experience on how to bring us up. I never got a hug from my dad. I have no recollection of ever having a hug from my dad. That was how he was brought up. Totally zero hug. Much harder than how I was brought up. He didn't have a father; he had to provide for himself—from the time he came out of the womb almost. Talk about survival. Things were rough. People don't know how bad things were.

Then the Second World War over there—it was bad. It was bad, but even then he always managed to put food on the table. Flour, salt, sugar, things like this were very hard to get, but my dad always managed through the black market—he even provided other people with flour and salt and sugar through the black market. He worked very hard, like I said—Rescia. He was an entrepreneur and a real provider. We had a place to sleep and food on the table. His own father didn't do that for him, but he didn't turn his back from his family or his responsibilities. And even if he didn't know how to hug us, he did love us very much. I love you, Papa.

I did have some school, a few classes here and there, but I inherited my common sense from my dad—a tremendous amount, without patting myself on the back, I have tremendous common sense. I can figure things out. Don't get me involved with a computer or a cell phone (although I use both). I learned a lot through my dad. He never went to school a day in his life, but still he was my teacher. Many times he would teach us through some spanking that we got. I would often get a spanking that I didn't even deserve, unjustified, because I was the biggest one. My brother Peter, he would get a spanking, and then he'd run away. He'd disappear for three or four days; they couldn't find him. My brother Mario was not spanked as much because he was small, anemic, not as healthy. (You would never know that of him today. He grew up to be known as the Mountain Goat of Montana because of his mountain climbing. You can read about it in his book, *The Mountain Goat Chronicles*.)

Once, when I was around five years of age, my younger brother Mario and I went upstairs and found a huge bottle of grappa and cherries; the cherries were very tasty with the grappa. It had a very high alcohol content, too. We really didn't drink the grappa, but the cherries were soaked in it and we probably ate a couple dozen each. So we, being kids, were playing around and I said to Mario, "Let me give you a shave." With what? We were playing with my dad's straight razor. Well, I cut like this and put three huge cuts down. Of course, he screamed. My mother came up and I'm sure it frightened her, and she called for my dad. Of course, he reacted to that and kicked my butt downstairs. My mother intervened, and I remember my grandmother, Caterina, was yelling at him. But, boy, did I get a beating that day! That is the only negative thing I have to say about my dad. And of course, Mario still has the scars from what I did, so it was a pretty serious thing and I can understand why he reacted to the situation the way he did.

In the early 1940s, my dad bought a little hotel in Berbenno, called Albergo. It is still there today. At the time, it only had a dozen rooms or so and a small restaurant, or trattoria, with bar-type food. Our town only had four or five hundred people, so it didn't really need a hotel larger than that. Our family ended up living there because we had so many rooms in there. We had a kitchen way down below, like a basement, where Caterina, our nonna, our grandma, she'd be working down there doing the cooking, helping out. Us kids would be down there helping our nonna. My mother would be working at the bar. People would be playing cards or playing *morra*, a game of chance. Customers would make a lot of noise playing *morra* and drinking. My dad would be at the hotel there doing various business and trading and buying and selling real estate.

Another thing my dad had going on was cutting small trees in the forest and cabling them down. He would buy a small wooded piece of land and hire some people to cut down the trees. The men would cable them down from

Hotel Albergo as it looks today

one hill to the next hill to the next hill. The trees had to be brought down the hills in a zigzag because, of course, going straight down the mountain, they could lose control and crash the load. Then us kids, especially me being the oldest boy, we had to carry the wheel, the *gilere*, which we used to cable the trees down the mountain, back up the mountain on our backs in a special cushioned burlap-type sack that had a strap that went around our foreheads. My dad would take the trees in his little old truck and sometimes with a mule or horse with the wagon to sell them.

We were all a little sickly—anemic when we were young. I remember there was a small epidemic of TB going around, and my parents were concerned I might have TB. The butcher in town, whenever he'd kill a cow, maybe twice a month, he'd have to drain the blood and he would catch some in a mug for me to drink. Of course the butcher saved everything. Nothing of the cow was wasted. The blood was hot, sweet, and foamy. No one else in my family, if I recall correctly, would drink it—there would be hair in it—even without that, it isn't that appealing.

When I would milk the cow, I'd put my stool down and hold the bucket between my knees. I'd clean off the cow teats by rubbing them down and getting any dirt, poop, or whatnot off of them, and then I'd milk the cow. Sometimes my parents would comment, "Oh she didn't give that much milk today," because while I was milking her, I'd lean over and shoot some milk into my mouth—sometimes even a quart or so worth. (Today we call it "latte.") This is another thing that probably helped me get healthy and maybe the reason I have such good teeth even to this day.

My dad would buy these old clunky mules and horses. They could barely stand, poor guys. But I tried to feed them and take care of them, give them water—the best I could. We had a friend of our family, of my mom and dad, and he had a business and this beauuutiful stallion. Wild, ohhh, well fed, well groomed. Oh, I wanted that horse so bad, and I told my dad. I says, "Dad, why don't you buy a horse like that sometime to work with? Not only will it work hard, but it would give me pleasure to have an animal like that—strong."

Well, he didn't buy a horse, but he did buy a young mule. Young, gorgeous mule. Strong. I was using that mule, a lot, a lot. That mule and I, we got along. I would talk to him; I would feed him. God, he would pull.

I remember on one occasion, I took our mule and a wagon for some sort of delivery or pickup down to Milan way below Bergamo, and I fell asleep in the wagon and then I woke up and didn't know where I was. Well, my dad had bought this mule from a little town way far away from our house, and the mule, he remembered his old barn, and he took me to the barn. Most horses were so well trained that they knew how to go home, so if you dozed off a bit, they would manage to stay to the right and get you home, and that is just what this mule did. Of course, there was very little traffic, maybe another wagon here or horseman there. Needless to say, I was late getting home that day by nearly five or six hours. Boy, were my parents worried!

My dad was doing pretty good prior to the war; we had some stoves that burned wood, even charcoal. We had a mule, a horse, a couple of cows, a couple of sheep. Then he bought a little old, old, old German truck, which had air tires, and a little Fiat truck, a French Renault truck—just junk really. Old. Old. Most of them had hard rubber tires and a little tiny door. They did have a little glass on the front. When we used to go and get a load of something, we used to freeze, freeze, freeze! Later all vehicles owned by the people had to be converted so they could run on a type of wood charcoal we made. We had no gasoline; all of the gasoline belonged to the government for the war. We also used a homemade grappa, which was made with the leftover grape peels, along with the wood charcoal—so it was true ingenuity. I even remember sneaking a taste of the grappa on those cold days to warm up a bit.

Chapter Four

The Second World War
1939–1945

As I record some of this, it is Pearl Harbor Day. When it happened in 1941, I was ten years old. I remember in Italy as a boy, it made big news. Right after that, war was declared and that is when the Second World War started. Of course, the Americans had their hands full for the first time. Here is a country that had to combat two opposite ocean wars overseas. So our navy had to be awesome, awesome, awesome. But so much of it was destroyed in Pearl Harbor. But because of how America was (not me at the time), we were able to come back from the death with a victory. Thought I'd mention that.

It was a terrible war. My dad, being an American citizen, was constantly hunted for this and that. In order to survive he had to appear loyal to Mussolini. One thing my dad did to show he was loyal to the Italian government and Benito Mussolini was to name my sister who was born at the time Benita. Another story, as I recall, was when my parents met with Mussolini in a big huge rally in Rome with many other people. They shook hands with him and had their photo with him. Later, my mother destroyed these photographs because when the partisans came to town they wanted to kill all that were involved with Mussolini, and she didn't want them to think they truly were loyal to Mussolini. They were invited to go down and meet him along with other families because Mussolini gave a trophy to the family who could have

I am the 2nd to the left in the uniform the youth were required by Mussolini to wear

more children in order to colonize. It was a dream of his to send more people down to Libya to control it because of the oil.

People knew my father was helping the U.S. and British, and of course some people really did not like that. They knew because he was an American citizen, he was not to vote in another country. (My sister Irene recalls men coming to our home and one pointing a machine gun at him and taking my father to vote. He raised his arms and said, "Who shall I vote for?" He lost his American citizenship because he voted that day.) Many years later when he came to America with his Italian passport, someone wrote to Governor Nixon and told him how my father was forced to vote against his will, and he restored his American citizenship to him.

During the war, there was a lot of killing, even in our small town. The Fascists would break in and take people away and put them to sleep forever. The Fascists were very brutal; they had been trained from a young age that everything was for the government. These were the Italian army of Mussolini. They wouldn't blink an eye to take your life away.

My dad had to join the Fascist Party for survival. But the opposition, the guerrillas or *partigiani*, they knew how it was with my dad; they knew he was an American citizen and what he really believed. Anyway, the guerrillas lived up in the mountains. They were good people; they banned together against the system. In those days, there was no GPS so they could really hide up in the mountains and in the caves; it was impossible for the Germans to go get them. You can't really get away with that these days.

We used to feed the partisans, the guerrillas, at night. They would come into town at night because they knew they would not be seen, and my dad and my momma would feed them, fix them a drink, give them wine—we had the restaurant.

My dad would have me drive the trucks when I was eleven or twelve, and we would go up to Navare, Asti, to get wine. Things like that. Many times there would be an American airplane, and they would come down in the plane like the Japanese did with those little fighters and try to machine-gun anything that was moving because they think that maybe you move fuel, gasoline, or food for the army. One time when I was in the little French truck, not very big, going to Asti with a convoy of three or four of us, this fighter saw us but we saw the plane coming, and we were able to stop and jump into a trench on the side of the road. It was maybe a foot and a half wide and three feet deep. He shot at us pretty good. We had big barrels of wine, and sometimes they thought we had gasoline. Your life is hanging on a string. We lost a little wine that time, but we could still drive. Some trucks got more damaged than others.

We had a garage, and one time the Fascists came and wanted to know if my dad's truck was in there. I told them, "No." One man grabbed my ear and almost lifted me off the ground and shouted at me, "Are you telling the truth?" And then they opened the garage and there was no truck.

Another time the Fascists, the SS were chasing me and this other boy. We were running for hours. At one point I tripped on a Coke bottle, and at that moment when I fell, they fired their guns and the boy that was running with me was shot through the head. I had to keep running. I jumped up and kept going.

My dad was often wheeling and dealing, going to the city to get a little this or a little that or buy some wine for the trattoria, you know, negotiating. And there was always some checkpoint you'd have to go through to go down to the valley. You had to have your paperwork to show the Fascists, the Germans. You could not just go through a checkpoint without it. They had a machine gun and everything. I mean, you blink your eye wrong and they shoot you. They'd raid a town and go through your whole house to find anything discriminating to haul you away. There was no news media to cover anything. They would kill the news media if they reported something they didn't like. It was just the way it was.

There was a man from our town, Barbone. He was called this because he had a long beard that went down almost to his knees. He was a mole for the SS. He would watch and listen. One time, I remember when the SS, the Fascists, came to raid the town, and my dad climbed up our chimney and hid. Barbone had told the Fascists that my dad was a double agent, which he was; he pretended to be loyal to the Fascists, but was helping the opposition. My dad would give some information to the British about how and when the fuel would travel down to the tanks in Africa. But someone told my dad that the Fascists were coming for him so he knew to hide. My mom was pregnant at the time, and there were maybe eight of us kids there. She had to answer the door and tell them that my dad had left. And they believed her. We didn't even recognize him when he came back down the chimney because he was so black. Of course, we didn't scrub the chimney all the time.

I had made a case, as big as a suitcase, out of wood with some letters on it, and I had a padlock on it. Well, one of the SS was going to take the case, but my grandmother told them, "Oh, that's the kids'. We lock their toys up in there because they fight over them." But I actually kept two, three hand grenades in there that I found in the hills. Man, what would have happened if they had taken the case and saw those grenades in there?

There were few Fascists that lived in our town that I knew of. They stayed undercover because of the guerrillas. But the guerrillas found out about this

Barbone. They came down and picked him up and took him way out in the forest and killed him and left him to be eaten by the animals and the birds. I was out one day to do an errand for my dad, maybe to take a telephone message to someone way far up in the mountains—ten, twelve miles. It was Passover, Easter. In Italy, Easter is a big holiday. Maybe even bigger than Christmas. Anyway, there was a nice working trail where the mules went back and forth and also a tiny shortcut—little animal trails that are traveled over all of the time and I took to come home. Of course I was young, and I could run like a rabbit. And coming down through the little trail I came to a place that was a little gulch or something, and I am ready to make a little jump to leap to the other side, and I saw the body underneath. They had left Barbone's body out there on the trail. There was this big huge thing crawling out of the ears, the nose. Maggots, everywhere. Lucky I didn't have the diarrhea cause I would have pooed my pants. When I touched the ground, I took off like a rabbit to get to the top of the mountain where my dad and everybody was, and I told everyone because they hadn't seen Barbone in about a week. Someone went and cleaned up the body and buried him or something.

Now on Sundays we would go to the Catholic church and have a special service during which the priest goes up in the pulpit and tells you about the Bible, the history, God, and this and that. It is a good time for everybody to take a nap because you fall asleep. On one particular day, my dad invited a cameraman to take a picture of our family. Remember back in those days, the cameraman would cover himself up and squeeze the thing, whatever it is called, and you would hear a pop. Just about the time the pop went off, we heard this explosion a mile down from where we took the picture.

Well, there was some bird's nest there. We used to go and get the nest, and just before the birds would fly away we'd catch the birds and take them home and eat them. And you know, we were hungry; we ate anything.

My friend Pierino was down there looking for the birds and found a grenade. If I was there, he would have said, "Hey, Battista, look what I found." And I would have said, "Don't touch it! Don't touch it!" because I knew how to handle the grenades and how dangerous they were. But he was playing around, and it blew up in front of him. It cut his chin up, his arms, he was bleeding too bad. He was thirteen, but he was a strong boy, well fed. That family had a couple of cattle and meat and things. The first lady that got to the explosion was his mother. She was in her late fifties or early sixties—this child was born in her late forties. She was a huge woman, sturdy stock about six feet tall. She picked him up and carried him about a quarter mile to the house. He was slapping her with his arm—it was just moving, he couldn't help it. He was covered in blood. He was screaming; he couldn't talk because his chin was gone. Some of his vocal cords were cut. He was mooing like a cow. We must have been forty or fifty people standing outside the window listening. We had a butcher in town, no doctor. The butcher came and put a pillow on his face and suffocated him because he wasn't going to live. Helped him from suffering more, you know. Pierino his name was.

Pierino had a brother. We thought my sister Giovanni and he were going to hook up, but they never did. He went to Switzerland, just a bit north, through the mountains to sneak in just like the Mexicans sneak into the United States through the desert. Only people sneaking into Switzerland have to go through the mountains and run into a lot of snow. There were half a dozen others with Pierino's brother, and he is the only one who survived. The others all froze in the high mountain. There was a St. Bernard that found them. They did have a little cabin up there, a little rock; they didn't make anything out of wood, everything rock, you know. He was a sturdy boy. Yeah, I remember him.

The American airplanes, the B-24, B-17, they would come up and bomb Milan a lot; it was a big industrial city. And down the valley from Berbenno, there was a main railroad for hauling military supplies. Once they came in and bombed the railroad. The bridge was damaged, but I had just passed; I think I had been going by with my mule and some wine to deliver. I didn't get hit, but a sheepherder and a boy and his family, they got hit. They weren't even the target.

Another time they were using the machine guns, and a stray bullet hit my mule in the ear. It was a close one for me.

At the end of the war, people celebrated for weeks. There still was no food, no this, no that, and we still had to rebuild—but we had more freedom. We didn't have to worry about the Germans, the Fascists to come to our houses. We were free!

Many months later, the U.S. sent wheat and all kinds of supplies to Italy. The winters up north are very harsh. We used to see all the American products, mainly food, clothing, and blankets, in the stores, but we didn't have money to buy them. These things was supposed to be given to the people.

Chapter Five

Switzerland
1945–1949

Things were really bad in Italy after the Second World War. My dad pretty much lost everything. So he decided to send me to Switzerland to work. Once again, this is about the same as people coming into America from Mexico to get work over here. I was about fourteen at the time. I remember it was summertime. In order to get in, you needed to go through the proper channel. One time we tried to go through the mountain, but I never made it because there was too much snow. So my dad was good about trying to get all of the paperwork taken care of and all of that. It wasn't a passport, though. I didn't have any cousins or relatives who went with me, so my dad sent me along with other married men from Italy.

We took the train from Milan. A real choo-choo, the one that runs by coal. I made a stupid mistake of sticking my head outside the window, and a piece of coal dirt went into one of my eyes. Boy, that thing stuck in there for about twenty-four hours. Drove me crazy. A lady on the train said to me, "Don't rub your eye or you are going to do more damage." She told me to wash it out with lots of water. Well, there was no water on the train. When we stopped I was finally able to get some water to wash it. After a day or day and a half, I was finally able to clear it out.

When we arrived, we had to go through a special disinfection because we were full of lice. We never showered; we had no way to in Italy. We didn't even have soap when we did, so yes, we had a lot of lice in Italy. I don't know, maybe once a month we heat the water for the tub. There would be the whole family. I being the biggest boy went last. And I imagine everyone wash their butt and pee in there and all of that. So it was cold soup by the time I got in there. So yes, when we got to Switzerland, we were pretty dirty and had the lice. The one thing the Swiss did not want was our diseases, so they disinfected us good. We went through three or four different rooms like a cattle drive. They gave us a shower, cleaned us, and sprayed us with a powder of some type. They put a mask on you and spray your ears, armpits, your coolo, your vagina, your testicles, depending on whether you a man or woman, and your feet—everything. Then I remember they gave us a little bit of clean clothing. At the station there were Swiss people waiting for workers, and I got connected with the Confair, trucking company, in the French section of Switzerland called Grandson near Lake Neuchatel. Of course, Switzerland has a German section, Italian section, a French section. I think maybe I end up with them because my dad had some sort of connection with them. I remember when I got there, the three big bosses kind of looked at me and said, "Oh my God, what did they send us here?" You know, because I was a little eighty-five-pound lad.

These people were the most wonderful, wonderful people to work for. They treated me like a king. I think they felt kind of sorry for me because I was so small, but they didn't know I was full of piss and vinegar and lots of common sense. Instead of me having to sleep in the barn full of roughneck people and other men, Italian, French, other people looking for work, they took me in and gave me a private room in one of the big homes. They fed me bread and jam and milk and croissants for breakfast. They even let me bathe in their back bathtub. I got to use a real bathroom instead of an outhouse. I bathed there once a week—every Saturday night when I came home from work. I was so dirty I could leave a ring around the bathtub easy. So I always cleaned after myself real nice. I wiped down the bathtub thoroughly. I didn't leave water on the floor. My mother always told me to try to be clean, to leave things in better condition than how you found them. If you take something out, put it back where you found it. I was very grateful to them, and I was sure to do as my mother had taught me.

The people I worked for could see right off the bat that I was very handy at driving. I could look at most anything: truck, car, Caterpillar, and make it go. I remember one time, one of the bosses looked at me and said, "Hey, Botch"—he called me "botch" or "little boy" because I was so small—"Hey, Botch, can you move that tractor and trailer full of logs there?" He was just joking around, but before he even finished his joke, I opened the truck and started it right up and asked, "Where would you like to have the truck?" He told me to take it across the street; it was a big plaza. So I took it there and hopped out of the truck. There were a handful of people walking by, and I heard them comment, "You see the little kid driving the big truck? He couldn't even see out the window." I knew what to do because I had seen the

Me at left, driving the Caterpillar

driver before and how he started it and put it into gear. The big boss was really very impressed.

Also working for the same company was a man whose job was driving the Caterpillar. He was a real maverick, a roughneck, and he did a lot of things and took a lot of chances. Eventually he flipped the Caterpillar over, and he was killed. Horrible. When they fixed the Caterpillar back up, the big boss says, "Battista. Botch. Can you drive the Caterpillar?" "Sure I know how to drive it." Once again, I knew because I had seen the guy start it up. So I took the job knowing they'd pay me more money. I'd drive up to the mountains and tow the logs out of the forest to the road with the Caterpillar. Every day someone would deliver food to me in the mountains, and then on Friday someone would come to pick me up or I'd drive back down with the guys in the logging trucks.

I had the opportunity to even drive the horses to pull logs out of the forest. They had beautiful horses, draft horses, well fed and groomed. The Swiss people took good care of their horses. Four of those horses has as much

One of the delivery trucks we used

power as a Caterpillar. Once in a while a Caterpillar had to be in for service, or someone would be sick, so they'd say, "Botch, can you work with the horses?" I loved to. I usually had only one or two horses because there was very little room to maneuver through the forest.

Once when I was maybe fifteen or sixteen, I had a horrible, horrible pain while I was driving the Caterpillar. I thought I was dying. I drove the Caterpillar down the mountain a bit to a pit stop like a little trattoria. Someone called for help for me there on their telephone and helped me get to the hospital. It turned out to be appendicitis. I was a very sick boy. I ended up being in the hospital for two weeks, on bed rest. At the end of the two weeks, my legs had to be bandaged so I could walk.

On the logging trucks, in those days, there was a little metal seat behind the wheels of the trailer under the logs where I would ride and help steer the truck. If I put my fingers down I could touch the ground, the seat was that low to the ground. Then I had this little wheel to steer the back trailer tire in order for the driver to make the curve. The rear driver would help him turn like a horseshoe. You had to be very careful not to hit the buildings as you came around corners. It was really terrible; smoke and mud would get in your face sitting back there. You had to drive very slow.

In the winter we could not go in the mountains because the snow was so high. Instead we would deliver wood and coal to various businesses, hotels, hospitals, and different places. We had special bags made out of a strong material like burlap that we'd fill with anywhere from sixty to eighty pounds of wood. I forget exactly how much we'd fill it. Then when we'd deliver it we'd have to carry it to the second or even fifth or sixth floor sometimes because most the furnaces were on the top of the building. We'd work all day doing that. Sometimes coal or this special gravel would come in with the train, and then we'd be at the train with a shovel as much as twelve hours a day. Really full workdays. We'd shovel the coal out of the car and into the trucks and then take the trucks to make the delivery. It was a pretty good-size company; we did a little bit of everything. They are still going strong today after over a hundred years.

Many times, even though I didn't even have a license, they let me drive their car, and I took all the lunches, delivered messages to the foreman, deliver this and that. I could do anything when it came to driving. I was a very handy young man, young kid. I did whatever they needed me to do. I learned French pretty fast because they didn't speak anything but French.

Even though I was there to work—I still had the occasional free time. There was a beach or lake there, which was quite cold. But there were a couple of months in the summer and these ladies would go there to bathe with no top on. And boy, my eyes really fell out of my head. Of course, in Italy you didn't see that, not with the very conservative Catholic religion. The French were much more open to that.

I remember there was a theater in a little town, Yverdon-les-Bains, and I would walk there seven, eight miles and back again just to see a movie. I wouldn't be in bed until midnight, and I had to get back up and ready to work around five in the morning. But this is how I saw some of the Roy Rogers, John Wayne, and other cowboy movies. All of the movies were in English, but they had French subtitles. I also saw *Frankenstein*, and I remember seeing Maureen O'Hara in *Buffalo Bill*. I was most impressed by that movie.

I worked six and a half days a week. I'd go to the movies Saturday nights, and then get up on Sunday mornings, and I'd wash my boss's cars—three big, beautiful cars—and vacuum them and brush out the carpet and then go to the movies again that night.

Sometimes they'd have a little circus in town, and I got to ride the little machine once in a while. Not much though. The money I made, I sent home to Italy.

I learned a lot from the people in Switzerland. I really hated to leave because I became part of the family. I was there from fourteen and a half until I was eighteen and didn't see my parents at all during that time. But I have to say, these people took me in and really took good care of me when I was a boy working for them, and I've never forgotten that. I kept in touch with Jean Jacques, the son of my boss, until he passed away recently at the age of eighty-seven. Over the years, I've made an effort to go to Switzerland to visit. The last time we met, Jean Jacques and his family came to Las Vegas, and I took the whole family, maybe eight or ten of them, to the best restaurant and paid for everything. One time they came to Las Vegas I got them a pilot, Robbie, and my Golden Eagle airplane to fly them around the Grand Canyon, San Francisco, and other places. I was so glad to be able to do this. They have a special place in my heart.

Chapter Six

America

1949–1952

One day my father writes me and says, "Battista, you need to come home. I'm going to send you to America. I found out you still have citizenship, but you need to go before you are twenty-one or you lose it." I had dual citizenship because my dad was born in America.

I went home from Switzerland in 1949 and stayed there about a month and prepared for my move to America. Giannina, Mario, and I went, and our cousins Adolfo and Sal, too. Some of them were much younger than me so there really was no rush, but my father had made contact with my grandfather over there, Pietro, and arranged for us to go.

We took the train either from Bergamo or Milan to the port in Genoa. From there we booked passage on the *Volcania*. It was the last of two old clunker ships, the sister ship being *Saturnia*. All of the others were lost during the war. The next day we hit the ocean. The Mediterranean was calm. We stopped in the famous Gibraltar Strait. We stopped there for a few hours, and the Portuguese came out to us in their little boats. They were selling cognac and little gifts to the people on the ship. We didn't buy anything because we didn't have any money with us.

After that rest the Atlantic Ocean was not too pleasant: big waves, big ocean, very excited. As my memory recalls, it took about two weeks to cross the Atlantic. The ocean got so rough. It wasn't a really super ship, but in those days it was still a pretty good-sized ship. The captain had to deviate us from our path for a few days to get to where they could hit the waves head on.

That first night we slept down below in bunk beds that were stacked two, three beds high. But the European passengers had been drinking and celebrating the day before, and in the morning, boy were they sick. I wasn't sick at all. I think some of my family may have been a little sick, but I don't recall. In the morning I went up to the dining hall, the mess hall, and there were big long tables that everyone in the ship could eat at. I'm telling you, I was sitting at a table maybe a hundred feet long and there was no one at it. There were maybe five people in the mess hall that morning. Everyone was down below vomiting, throwing up, this and that. So I had my breakfast, then I go downstairs and the sick people called to me, "Boy, can you go get me a Coke? A Seven-Up? Gazzosa? Candy?" Whatever it was they needed. Whatever sweet they had on board the ship to drink. And I'd be running back and forth between the people and the place that the ship sold these things at. The people would give me money to buy it with and then give me a few pennies tip or even five, ten cents. I think I got a quarter a couple of times. At the end of this, maybe two-week, trip, I had about six dollars change in my pocket. That is all the money I had. We left Italy with nothing but some salami and fruit.

Once we got to Ellis Island, the customs agents took many of our things away including our salami and cheese. I guess they didn't want any type of contamination.

We took a train from New York to California. I remember coming across the Rockies by way of Reno and a mega snowstorm hit. We got snowbound for a couple of days, and of course, we had no food to eat. But I did have that change in my pocket, and I remember a lady would come around the train with a basket of sweets and things to sell. And even when people ran out of money she still kept on going around working.

The train was parked on a curve and when the wind blew we could smell the steaks and hot food cooking in the dining car. And we were so hungry. I took the five of us—Gianinna, Mario, Adolfo, Sal, and myself—to the dining car and we sat down. We couldn't read the menu, so when our server, I recall he was a fine black gentleman, came to take our order we just pointed to different things on the menu. There were sugar cubes in bowls on the tables, and I remember we emptied them off several of the tables to eat later—not what you want to eat! Then our big meal came. I remember we ate so well. We even had wine. Our bill came to about sixty-five dollars or so, and when it came time to pay, I emptied my pockets to show our server we had no money. His eyes got real big; he went to call the maître d' of the dining car over. When the maître d' came over, guess what? He was an American who had fought in Italy during the Second World War. He was a captain or something and the Italians had taken good care of him while he had been there. So he took good care of us and took care of the bill. He says to us, "You can come back and eat once a day, but of course, we'll feed you what we have and not what you want."

Our train arrived in Oakland; it was New Year's Eve 1949, nearly 1950. Everyone was singing, drinking, partying, having a good time on the train. Many people traveling on the train were soldiers headed home.

I believe Grandpa, Pietro Locatelli, he was there waiting for us. He was driving a big Dodge sedan that I ended up purchasing from him several years later. We had very little luggage to carry. We left Italy with just the clothes on our back and maybe a little bag or something. We stopped in Los Gatos to meet some of the other Locatellis. These were several families that had immigrated to America in the late 1800s and now had successful businesses. Then we went on to Santa Cruz, and we stayed there with Nonno, Grandfather. The boys slept in the barn, which had a little simple apartment in it, and Giannina stayed in the house. Our cousins Fiorindo and Lupo (whose real name was Battista and was also called Battisti because of his small size) had come about six months prior to us, but I believe they stayed with their dad, Oreste.

Within a couple of days of arriving I got a job up the coast working for the Phiffer brothers. I think perhaps Lupo introduced me to the brothers. They had quite a few ranches, and they put me in a ranch not too far up from Santa

Cruz. They were all Italian except for the owners, who were Swiss, but Mr. Phiffer, he married a Locatelli, so there was a little bit of Italian blood in there.

My job was to go pick broccoli, sprouts, artichokes, whatever there was to be picked—we raised around three different crops—with the Filipino and the Mexican in the fields. There would be thirty, forty people, and we would pick and throw the vegetables into this custom trailer that the tractor would pull slowly up and down the field. We would walk alongside the trailer. Then a truck would come and pick up the full trailers and bring back an empty one for us to load. So we worked all day bent over, dawn until dusk, ten, twelve hours a day. The vegetables would be taken to a packing plant in Santa Cruz to be cleaned and prepped for shipping.

My cousin Battisti and I shared a little tiny room. I had one towel that I'd dry on the line after using, and I had to wash my clothes by hand and dry those on a line as well. There was a shower there for all the workers to use.

In those days, when they wet the fields they didn't have the sprinkler system like they have now. They ran a ditch at the head of the road and run the water down. Men would be standing there, and if the ditch would break, the men would put more dirt there to keep the water going. Then they would open up lines to where they plant the crop so the water could get to it. The tractors would also make little ditches where the plants were to be planted.

Well this one time, about twelve days after I started working, the man driving the Caterpillar got it stuck when he was pulling the trailer to where we were picking. There was another Italian guy, who was the big boss trouble-shooter—a foreman. He'd run up and down to the different ranches, make sure things were running smoothly, and if there were any problems, he'd stop to help. So he sees the Caterpillar is stuck and says he is going to go out to the main plant to get another truck to bring a Caterpillar to tow the stuck Caterpillar out. Unknown to any of them, I drove Caterpillars in Switzerland, but I didn't know any English besides "son of a bitch" so I asked the boss in Italian, "If I can get this Caterpillar out of here without you having to get a truck to tow another Caterpillar to tow this one out, which will take three hours, will you give me the driving job?" They were laughing, but I told them, "I am a very capable driver. Trust me; give me fifteen minutes and I'll have the Caterpillar out." Within the first three days of me working there, I had learned all about this Caterpillar: how to start one, how turn it off, how to use the tow cable—I had a lot of interest in it. To start the engine you pull the rope like a little lawn mower. To stop you disengage it and shut off the gas engine. Obviously it is called a Caterpillar because it crawls like a caterpillar. Whenever you drive one on soft ground, you put it in lower gear and let it idle and it can work itself out of anything. In my fifteen minutes, I dug under it with a shovel; it had already ruined some of the plants, so I put some of them under the Caterpillar tracks. Then I disconnected the three trailers (they move smoother through the wet spots and don't get stuck when they are separated), started the Caterpillar, and drove it right out. Where the Caterpillar had dug ruts in the soil, I filled them with dirt and leveled them off. I cleaned everything up real nice in fifteen minutes and showed my boss I had common sense. After that, I went and attached the three trailers back again to the Caterpillar and climbed back up in it. The guy says to me, "Whatcha doing there?" I replied, "Hey, I told you if I can get the Caterpillar out within fifteen, twenty minutes and you don't have to go get another Caterpillar to pull this one out, that I got the job." And this little old man, a nice old guy named Marcuchi, stood up for me and said, "Hey, you promised the kid." So the boss asked me, "You know what you're doing?" And I said, "Yes, I just go back and forth and I am not going to get the Caterpillar stuck again." When I saw a wet spot, I knew to disconnect the trailer and move ahead slowly and then come back with the cable and move them down. So I got the job. Not only that, but they put me in charge of all the driving at that particular farm. I was in charge of driving the trucks inside the ranch; I could not go on the highway until I got my license to drive. But I drove all of the trucks inside the ranch and brought the stuff up to the road. They showed me how to cultivate, plow the field with the Farmall tractor because after you pick the crop you have to turn the soil over. Man, was I in heaven.

My first month there I made 538 dollars. That would be like 5,000 dollars today. I worked an average of fifteen to eighteen hours a day. How did I do that? I got up early at about three in the morning and got the farm started. I would go out spraying pesticides, spraying with the Farmall to kill the bugs that would eat the lettuce and kill the sprouts. We wore no masks, nothing; we knew nothing. The reason we sprayed at night was because there was a fog from the coast that would bring a lot of humidity, and then the spray would stick to the plants better. I would finish around six in the morning, go shower because of the spray, eat breakfast, and then go back out to the fields and drive the Caterpillar. We would come back covered in dirt, just black with dirt. The shower we used had some wood slats in the bottom. Ten to fifteen people could shower there. So I did shower every night. They had outhouses for us, with a poop shoot and all of that. At night the lady there would have a beautiful dinner for us. The cook, she was from Switzerland. Then I would go to bed and sleep five or six hours and be back up again at three in the morning. I was a busy boy. I always worked six days and sometimes seven. That first month I really pushed it. I worked there about two years and always sent some money home to my parents. We got paid once a month, and I remember the prostitutes would come every payday for the Filipinos and Mexicans that worked on the ranch.

I purchased a 1939 Ford Coupe with the money I saved. It was a small two-seater with a V-8 engine. I dressed it up real nice. I thought I was a hotshot. It had these exhaust pipes with a muffler that made it really roar. A police officer pulled me over and gave me a twenty-five-dollar ticket. I had no idea I would get a fine for that. Why would the auto shop sell me something illegal? I even told that to the judge, but of course, I still had to pay the ticket.

Once in a while I'd get together with a few of the people and go to the Moose Lodge and dance. I even bought myself a nice suit to wear out. One occasion at the Moose Lodge, in March of 1951, I met the most gorgeous, beautiful woman, Rio Bornholdt. She was working at the credit bureau and dating a nice-looking young man named Sonny at the time, but I still asked her for a dinner date and she said yes. But when I called her a day or two later, she told me she couldn't go. She had received a call from her aunt Francis in Pasadena that her uncle had died and she had to go stay with her. I thought she was trying to get out of our date.

So it was a year later, in March of 1952, that I saw Rio at the Moose Lodge again. And again I asked her for a date. This time she said yes, and we did go out on a date. I never dated any other girls besides Rio. I had one close female friend in Santa Cruz named Julia before I met Rio, but I don't think I ever even kissed her.

It was only a month later that I asked Rio to marry me. I didn't know how to get a wedding ring, so I asked Rio to pick out our bands. It cost me seven dollars and fifty cents a week to pay for it. It was shortly after that, on July 5, 1952, that we got married. Rio was born on October 22, 1931, so we were both twenty years old at the time we married, nearly twenty-one.

We were married in Reno at Rio's Aunt Ethel and Uncle Ben's home. Her Aunt Ethel played the piano, "Here Comes the Bride," as Rio walked down the hall. We had our wedding dinner at a small casino. There were ten of us.

Rio and me on our wedding day

Chapter Seven

Married with Children
1952–1955

When I married Rio, her father, Carl, was working in Anchorage, Alaska, painting Quonset huts. He was a painter most of his life, and he was in Alaska doing work for the government up there. So I didn't even meet him until after we were married. Because he was away, I asked Rio's mother, Florence, for Rio's hand in marriage. She said yes, but with a very serious lecture: "You better not ever lay a hand on her!" She, and many other people at the time, thought Italians were all a bunch of wife-beaters.

Shortly after we married, we drove Florence (Nanien) in a Ford station wagon up to Spokane, Washington. From there she took a boat to Alaska. We stood and waved as the boat departed. Florence worked in a photography studio up there for two, three years. Because Rio's parents were in Alaska, we sold the little house we had and went to stay in her parents' house, free living.

But before we returned to California, we went to visit Rio's aunt Charlotte, Nanien's younger sister. She was swell. It was roughing it there in Spokane. I remember staying in a small cabin with no toilets, only outhouses. But we were newlyweds and we didn't care; we still made love. We didn't have protection one time, and that is how Rio became pregnant with Pier Leigh. So this must have been in September and we had just married in July.

At the time we married, I had already found a new job working in Davenport, just west of Santa Cruz at the quarry with some of my cousins. Sonny worked there, too. It was part of the Santa Cruz Portland Cement Plant. My workday was ten to eleven hours including drive time. I made sixty-five cents an hour, which was good money. I worked with the jackhammer, drilling holes to blast the rock and the mountain. We drilled down as far as twenty-one feet with the jackhammers. Then we'd put seven or eight sticks of dynamite in the holes. It was hard work. I eventually became in charge of the dynamite because it paid a little more money. I was like my dad, a go-getter; if I can make a little extra money, why not?

Then way down below the quarry was a big tunnel and there were special gates that would open and pour rocks into the chutes that would fill the train cars below. Then the trains would take the cars to the plant that was about six miles away by the ocean. This was a special lime type of rock, limestone or something that they could make cement with.

My uncle Oreste; my dad, who came to America in 1953 for a several-year visit; Adolphe; and my cousin Fiorindo all worked there. As I said before, Fiorindo arrived in America six months before I did and started working at

the quarry and worked there his whole life. It was the only job he ever had and was there for forty, forty-five years, I believe. He was such a good, nice person. There is a not a bad word to say about him. He came down with Alzheimer's in his sixties and died from it.

Once when my dad was working in the rock quarry, he went to the bathroom out in the woods, like we all did, but when he grabbed some leaves to wipe himself, he unknowingly used poison ivy. He swelled up pretty bad down there; he had to go to the hospital. We can laugh about it now, but at the time it was pretty serious.

After the quarry mine, I went to work for Walter Schilling, at the slaughterhouse. They paid quite well there. Right away they put me in charge of doing all the killing, the cow, the sheep, the calf, the bull, everything. We could buy meat there for very cheap. So I'd bring steaks home, and we'd have a glass of wine. Boy, Rio and I were in heaven. Later on the slaughterhouse was sold to the Swift Food Company.

I always was doing something different; I was like my dad in that regard. I was never out of work, but I would move on to new things; that is how you learn. Why not?

When Carl and Florence returned from Alaska, we were still in their home in Santa Cruz. The house had a little apartment in the back of it; it was a little wing attached to the house. I believe Rio's older brother built it. So we moved in there with our first daughter, Pier.

Rio and I named Pier after the actresses Pier Angeli and Vivien Leigh. Our second daughter, Desiree's, name came from the 1954 movie with Marlon Brando and Jean Simmons called *Desiree* about Napoleon Bonaparte and his romance with a woman named Desiree. Down the road when Jean Simmons was married to Stewart Granger I had the privilege of waiting on them at the Bel-Air Hotel, and I told Jean Simmons I named my daughter after her and her role in that film.

My mother-in-law was such a wonderful, wonderful lady. She was always there to lend a helping hand. The best mother-in-law you could ever have. You know how people talk about their mothers-in-law, kind of a little spooky? I tell you that is not the case with my mother-in-law. If I didn't have a mother, she would have been my mother. I was very fortunate to have two wonderful mothers in my life. I learned a lot from Mrs. Florence Bornholdt. We came to be great friends until her last day. She lived to be just under a hundred. She had a very beautiful mind, very understanding, very open. I can't say enough kind things about her.

My mother-in-law and my wife discovered that I had a pretty good singing voice. I'd break out singing "O Sole Mio" or some Italian song. They'd say, "Oh Battista, that's a nice voice. You should do something with it." Next thing you know, I am taking singing lessons. I used to go down to Los Gatos, near Saratoga for my lessons. My instructor was a Dr. Bias, and he was blind. On a side note, across the street from his house lived the mother of Joan Fontane and Olivia de Havilland. Now at the time I was still working at the slaughterhouse, so I was able to pay for my lessons by delivering cow manure to Dr. Bias for his garden. He had a beautiful garden in his backyard. So I built a trailer and I'd hook it up to my car and get two or three singing lessons for a load of manure. He'd play the piano even though he was blind. This is how another chapter of my life got started.

I wanted to be a big star, go on stage. Some of it happened and some of it didn't. Mario Lanza was just coming to light then and Beniamino Gigli and others. I didn't have the money to go to school. One time we were going back to Italy to see if I could find a sponsor for school there because they thought I had a fantastic voice. I don't know if I did or didn't, but listening to myself now and to other singers now—it wasn't too bad. I think I could have become something big. I was kind of cute in my younger days. That helps too.

I had the opportunity to sing at Albert Hay Malotte's home in Hollywood. He is a well-known American pianist and composer. He wrote the music for "The Lord's Prayer." He dedicated that song to baritone John Charles Thomas. After I sang for him he said he would have dedicated the song to me if he had known me in 1935 because when he heard me sing it, he said I gave him goose pimples, the chills. Of course I was just a baby, a kid then.

They say sometimes certain opera songs belong to a certain voice, it fits the throat of certain voices. I think "Core 'Ngrato" was my song. It was written by two gentlemen, Salvatore Cardillo and Riccardo Cordiferro, both Italian, out of New York; they wrote a couple, or three or half-dozen songs, but "Core 'Ngrato" is the one that really stood out that people still sing today. Beautiful Neapolitan song.

Chapter Eight

Hollywood
1955–1962

When we came to Hollywood it was 1955. We went there looking for a job and a place to live because I wanted to pursue singing. Rio and I drove down with an old Jeep, old wagon. We left Pier in Santa Cruz. Rio's older brother Hill lived in Sun Valley and was upset when he learned we slept in the Jeep. But when you are young it is no big thing. We left Pier in Santa Cruz while I looked for a job and we found a place to live. I immediately started looking for work in an Italian restaurant. I drove up and down Sunset Boulevard to find a dishwashing job, busboy job—no one would hire me. How I got to the Bel-Air Hotel in Beverly Hills, I don't remember, but I went up there, and this was one of the most exclusive hotels at the time. At the time two of the most exclusive hotels in the world were the Bel-Air and the Beverly Hills Hotel.

So I went into the kitchen of the Bel-Air, and I bumped into somebody and told them I was looking for work. There was a man there named Jose Ramos; he was in charge of room service. Then there was Roberto Grajera, who by the way is still alive today and in his nineties. Jose Ramos asked me, "Did you ever work in a restaurant?" "Well," I told him, "my dad had a restaurant in Italy. I know a bit—how to clean a table and something." And Jose put me to work. Now I needed black pants, white shirt, black shoes. The only thing the hotel provides you with is the nice jacket in red or white depending on the department you work in. So Jose, very nicely—he didn't know me from Adam and Eve—he gave me the money to go buy the things I needed. Then the very day I started to work there, the union came in and asked for my name and said I had to join the union in order to work there, and it would cost me twenty-eight dollars. I didn't have the money. Jose paid the twenty-eight dollars for me to join the union. He called them, "You vulture sons of bitches." But that's the way the union was. So anyway, I joined the union, but it did pay off down the road; I got my money back from the union.

My first job at the Bel-Air was in the room service department. Room service was also in charge of the banquet department. We had banquets every lunch and every evening. In the morning we worked room service. I started my shift at five o'clock in the morning. I was always the first to arrive and the last to leave. I was a busboy initially, but they made me a waiter in no time at all because I learn fast even though I couldn't write English. But I would write the order for myself, and then I would go to the cook and explain this means this and that means that. There were a couple of big black ladies there that took a liking to me. They would help me; Ramos would help me to put down the order to turn into the kitchen, but most of the hotel guests would call their order in directly to the operator and the operator would take the order, and then a waiter would pick up the order and go deliver the food to the room. My eyes opened up real fast there. Here I am taking orders to Yul Brenner, Clark Gable, Elizabeth Taylor, Orson Welles, Stewart Granger, Sophia Loren, Gregory Peck, who I became friends with, and so many celebrities who stayed there. So many names I can't remember.

The Bel-Air didn't have any high rise—maybe two or three stories in some places. It mostly had beautiful bungalows spread out over the golf courses. In those days you could eat at the Bel-Air for two dollars and fifty cents to maybe three-fifty and have a New York strip steak with a bottle of wine and soup and salad. The price of gas was only about twenty-five cents.

We had a little house for us to live in there in Hollywood. I remember it was so hot there. There was no swamp cooler, and because it was between two apartment buildings, the breeze was blocked. Once we even slept on the porch because the house was so hot.

One time Pier got out of the house, and Rio couldn't find her. Of course she was very frantic. Someone had left the gate open in the yard, and Pier had wandered out unbeknownst to Rio. She finally called the police, and they said, "Yes, we found a little girl who matches your description. She was wandering down Sunset Boulevard. She is sitting on my lap having a doughnut." No charges were pressed. Once again, it was a different time.

I remember when James Dean died; he had just got done doing *Rebel without a Cause* with Natalie Wood and was working on *Giant*. Now every morning when you deliver breakfast to a guest, you always bring the newspaper with it. At the time we delivered the *Examiner* and the *Early Times*. Well, on this Monday morning around five or five-thirty, I was taking breakfast up to Tyrone Power because he had to be at the studio early to work on *The Eddy Duchin Story* with Kim Novak and the studio was sending a limo to pick him up. When I got to the room, I took the food out from under the rolling table, which had an aluminum box with thermal insulation to keep the food warm in, and I set the newspaper on top while I opened the table up in order for Tyrone Power to sit down and eat. On the front of the *Examiner*, big, red, bold whole page, "Jimmy Dean Dead" or something like that, and he saw the headline. He hadn't yet heard Jimmy Dean was killed. "Son-of-a-bitch," he said with his deep voice. "I was with him yesterday and he was showing off with his new Porsche and doing some stupid things with it, and I told him if you aren't careful that car's gonna get you killed." Tyrone Power was quite devastated.

Then around eight or nine in the morning, I brought breakfast to Henry Ginsberg; he produced the movie *Giant* with James Dean, Rock Hudson, Elizabeth Taylor, and many more. When Mr. Ginsberg saw the headline, he actually passed out, fell on the floor. I threw a glass of water on him and he came to. He says, "I had two and a half million dollars invested in this man. He was gonna be the superstar of superstars and he goes out and gets killed with a car. I cannot believe it."

At the Bel-Air Hotel, I waited on more movie stars and famous people. I met a lot of interesting people. I used to wait on Ronald Reagan a lot, even after he became the governor of the state of California. And the current governor of California, Jerry Brown—guess what? His father, Edmund Brown, ran for governor in the late 1950s, and I was hired by him to go sing, entertain people, when they had a convention. What a small world, a small world.

Speaking of a small, small world, I first met Conrad Hilton when I was working at the Bel-Air Hotel. He would throw parties at his home, sometimes with 150, 200 guests, that the Bel-Air would cater, and I would bartend for them. Unknown to me then, years later his son Barron Hilton and I would become really good friends—even going fishing together at Waterfall in Alaska. He, of course, is the owner of the Flamingo Hilton Hotel, which is behind the Hole in the Wall. I sold a piece of property behind my restaurant to him.

I waited on Grace Kelly and the prince of Monaco at the Bel-Air Hotel. Before they were married, they came in once for an early lunch, and they were there so long that all the other employees went home—they would come back for the dinner shift at five. So I stayed because someone had to stay to see if they needed coffee or anything. When they were leaving, I was wiping the booths off and out comes a roll of hundred dollars bills with between five and ten thousand dollars in it. I ran to the parking lot and the valet was getting the car. So I told the prince of Monaco, Prince Rainier, I told him I found his money in the booth. I thought he might give me a tip, but all he says is, "Thank you, boy." Not even "sir." Just "boy." But so be it. Big people with small minds. What are you going to do? You know what I mean?

The Bel-Air, as well as the Beverly Hills Hotel, La Scala, and other top restaurants, would cater for the celebrities, and I would often have the opportunity to go work in their homes for parties and events. I was a good bartender because I had personality and I sang and I could speak three or four languages, none of them good—but I could. Zsa Zsa Gabor, when she was married to Conrad Hilton, Paul Newman, Joan Woodward, are just some of the customers I recall. Now, my shift was all day with a two- to three-hour break between lunch and dinner, and it ended around eleven at night. I recall one night when I was finishing one of these shifts at the Bel-Air, the maître d' tells me that Shelly Winters lives up the road and would like me to go up and work as a busboy, waiter, bartender, whatever. So I went up and worked my ass off until five or six in the morning. We had no cell phone so I couldn't call my wife, and she was worried. At the end of the night, Ms. Winters gives me a couple of her clothes to take home and two dollars. It kind of sucks. You know? What you gonna do? Big people with small minds.

One time I was driving up a steep road, the same one the Bel-Air is on, and down comes another car, a big Continental. Well, the driver of the other car turns out to be Edmund Purdom, who was in town working on *The Student Prince*. He had just taken over Mario Lanza's role in the movie, and we were in front of Joe Pasternak's home (MGM's musical producer who produced *The Student Prince*). Edmund Purdom wanted me to back up so he could go by, but I told him no because etiquette and safety rules, et cetera, et cetera, say the driver coming down needs to go back up if someone needs to move because if a car reverses down the hill, he could lose control. Well, he didn't like that none too much. He got real angry and started to cuss at me. So I had a kind of crowbar in my car that I got out and I was going to hit his big Lincoln Continental with it, so he backed up fast and left. He wanted no bad publicity.

When Sophia Loren came over with her momma and her family to make the film *The Dolphin* with Alan Ladd, they all stayed at the Bel-Air Hotel in a couple of the bungalows. She told me, "Whenever other people serve me, I always have to wait so long for my breakfast, but when you serve me I get it so quickly." That was nice. I explained to her that for such a big order for seven, eight people, it takes the waiter extra time to put everything together to bring it to the room—at least half an hour. But I told her, "Ms. Loren, the MGM is paying the bill, but you sign the check and you leave only fifty cents." "In Italy, un dolores un tanta lira," she replied [in Italy that is a lot of money]. "I know, I know, but we are not in Italy. You should put five dollars at least here," I explained, because her check was twenty to twenty-five dollars for a very big breakfast for eight or more people, and we would be working just for her at least an hour. We'd have two rolling tables, a heater and more, and a fifty-cent tip for one hour of work was all we would earn. She was very receptive to what I said. "Oh my God. I apologize. I didn't know," she said so sincerely. She made up for it later.

Always looking for a new adventure, I went to work for the Beverly Hills Hotel. I waited on Elizabeth Taylor a lot at the patio of the hotel because she had a big bungalow suite she lived in with Michael Todd at the time. I waited on so many celebrities at the Beverly Hills Hotel: Jimmy Stewart, Clark Gable, Noah Dietrich, Howard Hughes, Yul Brenner, and many more. I must mention that while I was working at the Beverly Hills Hotel, I met Rod Serling outside at the pool. He had come in to meet Charlton Heston. At the time, he didn't have a pot to piss in. So I brought him out a sandwich, and we became very good friends. Later, he brought me on *You Bet Your Life* with Groucho Marx, *Hollywood Talent Scouts*, and *The Art Linkletter Radio Show*. Who would have guessed?

When Michael Todd died in March, 1958, I was bringing up lots and lots of coffee and sweet rolls to Tyrone Power's tower suite because there were eight to ten businessmen there. And the headline in the newspaper I was bringing up said Michael Todd had been killed in a plane crash. One of the men there says, "Oh my God. Michael Todd came to me to borrow ten million to do *Around the World in Eighty Days*." The film ended up grossing millions of dollars. The man continued, "I should have lent him the money, but I didn't."

I always seemed to be bringing a paper to a celebrity with bad news. I remember, in November of 1958, bringing Yul Brenner the paper that informed him that Tyrone Power had died of a heart attack in Spain. Mr. Brenner had a very deep voice, you know, and, in shock, he asked, "What happened?"

When I left the Beverly Hills Hotel, I went to work at the Sporting Lodge. I left because there was a maître d' there by the name of Rex, and he was very jealous of me because the owner of the hotel, Mr. Goldstein and his wife, they liked me very much. So Rex made things very rough for me, so many stupid things he did to me. So someone invited me to come work for them at the

Sporting Lodge in San Fernando Valley. It was a very popular place. People could fish for trout, catch them, and have them cooked right there.

It is funny how people's paths cross. Soon after I left the Beverly Hills Hotel, Rex got fired and came to the Sporting Lodge looking for a job, and he put my name down as a reference. The maître d' asked if I recommend him for the job, and I put in a good word for him. They hired him as a captain, but it was the captain's job to debone a fish, and he didn't know how. So Rex came to me quietly and asked me to show him how, and I did. We got along fine. I never hold grudges.

After Elizabeth Taylor married Eddie Fisher in 1959, she sort of got to know me a little bit; they would come into the Sporting Lodge as well as John Wayne, Jerry Lewis, many others.

Once when John Wayne and Ward Bond and some others were having dinner, there was another table of men teasing John Wayne about how tough he was and really didn't know when enough was enough. So he finally stood up and said to the guys that was egging him on, "Listen, pilgrim." And I swear he banged their heads together. Everyone—the other customers—applauded for John Wayne.

From the Sporting Lodge I went to work at the Brown Derby also in 1959. There was a real jerk of a man there who was the food checker. He made sure the plates went out right and the tickets matched up with the pay. One day while I'm working, it was announced over the PA that Mario Lanza had died. It was such a shock for me. I had served him so many times. So I was in a bit of a daze over it, and the food checker asked me about some steak sauce. I said I didn't know what he meant, and he called me stupid. It was enough to ignite the fire—for me to blow my top. So I flipped the food tray I was carrying all over him, right there in the kitchen, and left—quit right there on the spot. But I wasn't out of work for any time; I called my friend Dan Tanner, who I knew was the maître d' at La Scala, and he got me a job there right away.

Also, Milton Berle's wife put a good word in for me with the owner of La Scala, a Frenchman by the name of Jean Leon. Once when I waited on her, there was a twenty-dollar bill sticking out of the cushions of the booth she was seated in. I saw it and put it on the table. I don't know if she planted it there on purpose or if it was truly an accident, but from that incident, I guess she could tell I was an honest guy.

One time La Scala catered an event for a political party June Allyson and Dick Powell were having in their home, and I went to work there as a bartender. I remember they were for Nixon because they had a picture of him on the wall, and it was a bit crooked—funny how you remember those sorts of things. Walter Cronkite was there covering the event and drinking a champagne cocktail. John F. Kennedy was there, and he came up to me and said, "Bartender." So I gave him my name, and we talked for about a minute, minute and a half, and I told him about Italy and this and that and of my dual citizenship. After a little chit-chat, he asks me, "Can you make me a drink, so that it looks like a drink?" So I says, "Sure." I told him, I says, "I'll give you some club soda with a little Seven-Up to make it sweet, and I put a squeeze of lime; it looks like a vodka Collins or a gin tonic." He says, "Great, 'cause I need to keep my mind alert and clear; it is so easy to have a little sip here, a little drink there, and I have to associate all day with so many people, I want to be sure I'm sharp. Thank you."

Marilyn Monroe came into La Scala all the time when she was making one of her movies. One of the men, a producer, he called and asked me to be sure Chef Pasquale only use skim milk in her fettuccine Alfredo to make it a little lighter. I remember the day she died. Rio and I were invited to lunch with Priscilla Kerr, the wife of actor John Kerr, and his mother June Walker. Priscilla had a part in an opera and had invited us over to meet a Japanese opera singer.

Katherine Hepburn would come into La Scala for an early lunch with Alice Faye, Betty Grable, Lana Turner. They'd stay and talk until three, four o'clock.

Sammy Davis Jr. would come into La Scala to eat. At the time because of segregation he wasn't welcome to stay at the same places as Frank Sinatra and Dean Martin and all the rest. But La Scala welcomed him to dine there. He was a very nice man. He even gave me a watch. I still have it today. It says "Mason" on the inside because he was a freemason.

When Gigli was born in January 1960, men were not allowed in the delivery room, so I was working. At the time I was bartending at La Scala and was talking with Robert Wagner and Natalie Wood, and I told them my son was just born, and I was thinking of naming him Rossano or Gigli, after Rossano Brazzi and Beniamino Gigli, and they told me to name him Gigli. So I called the hospital to tell Rio not to name him Rossano, since we had already decided on that. Well, there was no telephone in the room so Rio, just having delivered our son, had to walk all the way down the hall to talk to me on the telephone. "Rio," I says when she finally reached the phone, "his name is Gigli." And I hung up. I didn't know all the paperwork that had to be redone because of that. Years later Robert Wagner and Natalie Wood would come to the Hole in the Wall, and I introduced them to Gigli.

After La Scala I went to Casa D'oro. Lou Kaufman and Paul Logan opened Casa D'oro and asked me to come work for them. Paul Logan was the head bartender at La Scala, and I had worked under him.

I waited on Robert Mitchum many times at Casa D'oro. Once he cleared

Gigli with Robert Wagner and Natalie Wood

out the bar, he and Broderick Crawford. People were giving them some garbage, and a fight started. One of the owners, Paul Logan, came up to me and says, "Locatelli, why don't you stop him?" Well, these guys were 220 pounds. Me and my 148, 150? Come on! You sick in the mind? I says, "I ain't gonna stop him!" So Paul Logan went over there, and man, he got a punch in his mouth that he flew across the table and passed out. So he learned his lesson. He loved to drink, so he got up, he says, "Locatelli, make me a double martini. Triple it!" he says.

Chapter Nine

A Singing Career?

1962–1969

In 1962 we ended up moving from Hollywood to Santa Monica; I was hoping to get my singing career going. I landed a part in *Madame Butterfly* at UCLA and at Pasadena Gardens and a couple other places as Lieutenant Pinkerton. I also started singing at Bimbo's 365 club in San Francisco. Nelson Eddy performed there regularly. I had a chance to take over one of his shows, but he wouldn't let me have a nightly performance of my own. He was getting older, and I guess it worried him, the idea of someone younger taking his spot. But it all worked out in the end for me. God really had his hand on our family.

Over the course of seven or so years, I sang frequently, about every three weeks, at the famous Horn in Santa Monica. It wasn't a paying job, but in order to perform there, you had to audition. This is where Sammy Davis Jr. got his start and Jim Nabors, who went on to play Gomer Pyle, and many, many other no-names got their starts there. Alan Jones and I sang at the Horn together, and his son Jack Jones became quite popular as a singer in Las Vegas. Jack Jones would come into the Hole in the Wall when he was in town performing.

I needed a job that would free up my nights and weekends for singing, so for five or six months Rio and I worked for a Mr. Harbman in Santa Monica. We made car fender protectors and seat covers for mechanics to use while working on customer cars. Rio was doing the sewing at home with Gigli and

CHAPTER NINE

My daughters from left to right: Heidi, Pier, Desiree and my son, Gigli.

Heidi while Desi and Pier were in school, and I was doing all of the cutting, and I would go out and sell the covers. Mr. Harbman really liked my singing voice. And he said, "I am going to open another location back East and you and your wife can run it. You find a place, and I'll help you with your singing."

So Rio and I, Pier, Desiree and Gigli, and Heidi all moved to New Jersey. When we started looking for a place to live, a police officer stopped us and asked what we were doing. He told us we didn't want to live in the area we had been looking at and that we needed to go about thirty minutes "that way." We were a bunch of blondes that would have really stood out, I guess—a drop of cream in a cup of coffee. So we picked Avenel, New Jersey, first, and then later we went to upstate New York.

We found this nice little home and were standing outside admiring it when a young neighbor kid came over. He was in his early twenties and recently won some bodybuilding contest. He introduced himself as Stanley Winters, and we introduced ourselves and made some small talk. We told him we really liked the house, but it turned out the deposit was going to be five hundred dollars. We didn't have that kind of money, so we were going to keep looking for another place to live. He told us to wait a minute, and he ran back into his home. A moment later, he came back out with five hundred dollars cash. He just gave it to us, complete strangers. Who does that? We've never forgotten that. Never, never, never. We've paid him back over and over since then and are still good friends with him to this day.

I went to the Metropolitan Opera to pursue my singing career. They said I had a lot of potential but that I needed more training on the technical side of music—such as reading music. Because things never really moved forward for me musically and for a few other reasons, we moved back to California. We felt we really let Mr. Harbman down because he gave us a chance to make our dream come true.

When we came back to California in 1964, we briefly stayed in a one-bedroom apartment in Van Nuys, and then we got a nicer apartment at Sherman Oaks. I started driving school buses in San Fernando Valley. How stupid was this? I could have returned to working at the restaurants and hotels instead.

Well, I guess I did it so I would have more free time to sing on the weekends. Mom and I were both driving school buses. Rio sometime drove for special trips, the big bus, the crown; she was quite the driver. Burt Lancaster's children even rode her bus to and from school. She went from working a thirty-four- to a ninety-two-passenger school bus in no time. She picked it up real fast. Rio was something else, let me tell you. If it needed to be done, she was the lady to get it done. That was one thing we've never done in our lives is walk away from work. Neither of us. We did what it took to put food

CHAPTER NINE

In front of my bus

on the table, to pay the bills. Rio and I even painted houses for a couple of people, a friend of ours who was well-to-do, to help bring in a little extra money.

Anyway, driving buses, I became very popular. In the school buses, when we went home for Christmas, the front of my bus, it was full of presents. Other people just got a little thank-you, but I had presents—sweater, socks, jackets, and money—'cause I treated the kids right. I was good to the kids. They wanted to play the radio; they wanted to listen to this channel or that channel. I says, "You know what? Monday we listen to this channel; Tuesday we listen to that channel." And so on. Now everybody's happy. I had one bad boy, a little troublemaker, so I say, "You know what? I need some help. I need someone to be in charge to keep control on my bus." Well, my bad boy, he had a responsibility, and he become a superstar overnight.

Another time I had two boys who started to fight on the bus. So I stopped the bus and told them to get off the bus and fight. So they did. When they finished, they got back on the bus, and I continued my route. Can you imagine if I did that today?

I drove buses for the Associated Charter Bus Company when we lived in that apartment. Mom was the manager of the apartment. We used to take the trip to where the Dodgers played whenever they played in town. I took many trips down there. Saw many of the greats: Sandy Koufax, Don Drysdale, Willie Mays, Manny Mota—matter of fact, I have a baseball signed by Manny Mota. I was there the night that Drysdale pitched either the fifty-six or fifty-eight scoreless innings. Fifty-five or fifty-six thousand people at the Dodger Stadium—jam-packed. There wasn't a seat available, not even standing room anywhere. And Willie McCovey, when the last pitch was coming down the pipe for Drysdale, it was poor sportsmanship for Willie McCovey, he stuck the belly out to get hit on purpose, instead of to duck and put the belly in and let the ball go by. And of course, everybody stood up and booed him. The umpire called McCovey out. Then the crowd went really wild. Everyone cheered. Standing ovation. That is one historic play I was there for.

When we drove for the Associated Charter Bus Company we took tours all over Southern California: to Big Bear, Lake Arrowhead, various camps, and Disneyland. We were the first company to drive into Disneyland. We were able to bring our family, and we even ate in the cafeteria with the Disney park employees.

Double-decker bus I drove for Beverly Hillbillies

When driving the double-decker, I usually was dressed as a typical English driver, and I'd pick up the guests: entertainers such as Bob Hope, Sheldon Leonard, Buddy Ebsen, Carl Reiner, and the Smothers Brothers, to name a few.

I got to know Tom and Dick Smothers when I was driving charter buses. Once they had me dress as a beefeater. You know, the guy in the costume on the gin bottle. I have a picture of myself

In my Beefeater costume

Carl Reiner and me

in the costume in front of the double-decker bus. We have remained friends all of these years.

Carl Reiner was looking for a host for one of his parties in Beverly Hills, and he had seen me and been around my personality on the bus a little, and Tom Smothers told him what a good personality I had. Also, he told him I could speak several languages and sing and that I would be a perfect host and greeter for his party. So I got the job. I rented a nice suit and shoes just for the event.

I took the Girl Scouts on tours and businesspeople on tours of the aqueducts. Some of the big businesspeople, when they were building the aqueducts to bring water from Northern California down to Southern California, said, "You need to have Battista Locatelli take you." I'd take these special people, here and there. But it was good service. Service is the name of the game.

One time I was scheduled to appear on the *Regis Philbin Show* but I had a shift as a bus driver, so guess what? I wore my bus uniform on the show. There was no time to change. I sang two or three songs, "Core 'Ngrato" was one of them.

While we were living in Sepulveda, I went to work for the Shell Oil Company driving an oil tanker. Don't ask me why I wanted to do that. It must have been more money or insurance. I only worked four days a week for ten hours a day. So I had extra time to pursue singing. But I became very popular down there. There was a written test I was supposed to take, but I couldn't write very well in English, so they made an exception for me and gave me an oral exam. I passed with a 99 percent and only had one month of training.

We had to make many fuel deliveries; we had many compartments in the oil tankers. You know, you have high grade, low grade, and so many gallons at this station and so many at that one. Many of the Mexican stations, they didn't buy too much gas there; I'd pour five hundred of one kind and a thousand of another and go on to the next station. Those were private-owned stations, not like the big station like Shell and others.

One time at the main office, the guys tell me to watch out for this guy, this particular customer. They tell me, "He's gonna buy five hundred dollars worth of gas, then he's gonna count the money three, four times, and then you count it, and then he count it again, then you count it again, and he'll count it again; he wants to be the last one to count it. Finally, he'll say, "Yeah I got it right," and he'll cheat you out of a hundred dollars." He had already managed to cheat a few of the drivers for a hundred dollars. It was always one hundred dollars. So my last delivery on this particular day is to this man I was warned about and it also happens to be the same day I am supposed to leave for an audition—my big break—in Las Vegas with Harold Minsky. I was all anxious, in a hurry, like I am sometime—Mom is right—and I had to go into the office that night after my shift and deposit my money in a big safe deposit box. Because it was after five o'clock there was no one to personally record my payments received, so I put it in an envelope with my name "Tony Locatelli" and dropped it in the locked box. They called

SINGS — Battista Locatelli appears on Talent Scouts at 10 tonight (2).

CHAPTER NINE

During one of my appearances on the Regis Philbin Show

me Tony there because Battista was too hard for them, I guess, and Antonio is my middle name. Anyway, I was at the Burbank airport to take my flight to Las Vegas and they paged me there and says, "You came up a hundred dollars short from that last station delivery." Probably they think, I'm going to Las Vegas and needed the hundred dollars to buy a ticket. I says to them, "Well, I'm sorry. Just take it out of my pay. You know they warned me about this guy." And they said, "We know, we know you didn't take that money. We know that, but business is business, and you came up short." Of course it was my fault. So they took it out of my pay. Whatcha gonna do?

Now the audition took place in 1969 and was with Harold Minsky for a job as a production singer in Las Vegas at the Aladdin Hotel. Harold Minsky was the son of the man who started the burlesque clubs in New York, Chicago, Florida. The audition went very well. "Quit your job and move up here; we're starting rehearsals soon." So I called my big boss at Shell Oil, his name was Sean, and I told him I got the job at the Aladdin. He told me if I ever wanted my job back, "It's here for you." So I left on good terms.

After the audition, I returned to California and packed up my family and we moved to Las Vegas. I called Mr. Minsky every day and talked to the secretary. "Mr. Minsky is out of town, " she would tell me. "We'll call you back." So I waited one day, two days, three days, a week, I never got a call back. And so I moved on.

Later Harold Minsky became one of my biggest supporters when I opened the Hole in the Wall. He came in all the time, always bringing people with him. But he never brought up why he didn't call me back or why he lost the show. He didn't have the courtesy or maybe he felt embarrassed, I don't know the answer. I was a nobody; he could have had his secretary call and tell me the show fell through, go back to L.A., but he didn't, and it was the best thing that happened to me. Maybe he brought a lot of business to the Hole in the Wall because he felt guilty. Guilty or not guilty, we owe a lot to this man. We never would have done what we did if we hadn't stayed in Las Vegas. It was meant to be. It is funny how the chips, they fall into place sometime.

I did the best I could with my voice. I had a really great voice but it just never happened. Maybe I wasn't good enough, or maybe it just wasn't my time. I can say the work and the studying I put into trying to make my singing career succeed helped me move forward and succeed in the other career, the restaurant business. It did help. It forced me out of my shell, put me more out in the open to where I learned to talk to people to be a one-to-one personality.

Christmas morning with my children and the first of many electric toothbrushes.

I pretty much decided not to pursue a musical career after this. I had a good run. In the course of a decade I appeared on *The Art Linkletter Radio Show*, *The Regis Philbin Show*, *Arthur Godfrey's Talent Scouts*, on *You Bet Your Life* with Groucho Marx—some of these several times each. I performed countless times in clubs and on the radio. I performed in several stage productions of *Madame Butterfly*. These were all very special experiences for me. Through the years my voice helped me open many, many doors, but I never went nowhere as a singer.

Professional headshot taken for my singing career

Chapter Ten

A Restaurant Is Born

1969–1979

∽

I think it was June or July when we moved to Las Vegas. And boy, we were not used to heat like that. It was really hard to find a place to lease because of the kids—it wasn't a family-oriented town. Things were hard, really hard. We didn't have this; we didn't have that. We didn't have the money to buy a house. But guess what? My darling mother-in-law, Mamma Mia, Mrs. Bornholdt, she lent me the money. She was always there for me. We really became best friends. I did pay her back—all of her money, plus, plus, plus. She was always there for me to lend ten cents or twenty-five cents to make a phone call that meant life or death to my family. I've never forgotten that. I get tears when I think of Nanien. She was a fabulous, fabulous, wonderful human being.

So we bought this house on Arthur Avenue, and as I said, it was hot, hot, hot. There was no air conditioning, and there was no power. It was Fourth of July weekend and nothing was open. We had to sleep on the floors—completely bare floors, to where the nails were exposed. No carpet. Just a little memory. Later we sold that place and moved to Heritage Square.

A chef I used to work with in Beverly Hills, Pasquale Danza, owned his own restaurant in Las Vegas on Charleston called Cioppino's. I had worked with Pasquale at the Casa D'oro and La Scala. He was the chef at La Scala. A lot of locals, hotel owners, Bobby Darren, came in to Cioppino's—some musicians, some celebrities. For less than three or four dollars a person you got twelve ounces of the world's best New York steak, filet mignon, fish, whatever, plus wine and everything, everything.

So I went to work there for Pasquale and his wife, Virginia. I worked for tips only, but I made a lot of money because of my experience and what I learned from the Beverly Hills, the Bel-Air, La Scala, and others. It really paid off for me and my family. I made 125, 150, 200 dollars a night. Ask Rio, she remembers me coming home. Hell, I made more profit than the owner. I even sang for my supper. Haha. I sang many "Happy Birthday"s on many occasions. Sometimes people even requested a special song from me. It was very interesting; it was a very good job for me. Rio worked there for a time, washing dishes, doing this and that.

Pasquale and I got into arms a little bit, so I went to work for Cecil Lynch at the Little Caesar in a small shopping center on Tropicana. After that I started working for a Lou Cotanzaro as a waiter.

It was about this time that Rio and I started looking for a place to start a little restaurant. Now, Cotanzaro owned another restaurant called the Dive, and he was doing nothing with this place, and believe me it was a dive. It only sat fourteen people at the counter. There was a pool table, a couple pinball machines, an old house refrigerator, a little hot plate. Half the things there didn't work.

Joe Julian was the landlord of the shopping center that the Dive was in along with thirteen other shops. We took over Lou Cotanzaro's lease for the Dive and had to pay 320 dollars a month for rent to Joe Julian. We had a verbal agreement that I was to pay him $5,000 if I ever made any money. (He had left the furniture, refrigerator, two pool tables, pinball machines—all things he had paid for.) About a year later, I gave Lou $10,000.

When I first got the business license for the Hole in the Wall, I remember it was a really simple process. The sheriff at the time was Ralph Lamb. So I gave him the fifteen-dollar fee, and I had my license. You can't do that today. You have to be a millionaire already to start a restaurant and the paperwork is incredible. There is almost no such thing as the self-made man these days. Things are really terrible for someone who wants to start a business today.

We started our business when Las Vegas was just blossoming. We were at the right place at the right time. On May first, 1970, we opened the doors. We only served breakfast and lunch in the beginning. Right away we had quite a following; many of our customers were people I used to wait on at Cioppino's and Little Caesar.

At first, we changed the name to Trattoria, which is a name for a little type of restaurant in Italian. But it really was still a dive. There were so many cock-a-roaches. You could nearly rope them and ride them like a cowboy.

All this time, Rio kept her job driving school buses. She'd park the bus at the restaurant so she could make breakfast for the customers in between the morning and afternoon busing schedule. Sometimes when Rio wasn't there, I had the customers make their own eggs—I didn't know how to cook.

A man named Freddy came with the Dive too. He used to sleep there in a booth. He took care of the place. He could do anything. I insisted the floors be clean, and man, he could make them shine. He could fix anything; the man knew what he was doing. He worked for us for years. Later he worked as a bartender for a period of time. He was the greatest guy. Nice, nice guy.

I remember Barry Leydecker, who later married Pier, used to stop in for lunch with his dad, Bob, and his brother when they had their landscaping business. Barry would play pinball until he was blue. I guess he was pretty good because I had to pay him fifty dollars because he won. In those days if you won at pinball—a certain score—the owner of the machine gave the payout.

We really got started on a shoestring. At first we all worked there for nothing. The kids would turn in their tips. Everything went back into the restaurant. Of course, as they got older they got to keep their tips and got bonuses.

Right away, running the restaurant was a family affair. My brother Vittorio moved to Las Vegas before we opened the restaurant. He really helped us out. Mom did the cooking and the kids did some cooking, too. I was working eighteen to twenty hours a day, cleaning, singing, working as a waiter, a busboy, doing this every day.

When we first open the Trattoria, we mainly just cook hamburger, little things. Then this Italian gentleman who Vittorio knew started bringing us

Hanging a little something

Desiree with her nephew (Pier's son), Shawn in the kitchen of the Hole in the Wall

My daughter, Pier Leigh has done it all at the Hole in the Wall

pizza dough with sauce in the pans—the only thing we had to do was add the ingredients and put it in the oven. So we bought a little pizza oven to heat the pizzas. And whatever people wanted, we had the ingredients. Then Mom came up, or Mom and I, with the Dago Burger. We could get away with calling it that because I was a dago. What a big huge sell that was; it was one of our most popular items when we first opened. It was a hamburger with provolone, Genoa salami, shredded lettuce, and tomato slices served on a toasted bun that had been grilled with a thick garlic and olive oil spread.

Then I start to hang something inside little by little. I got a lot of these ideas from Pasquale's Cioppino. He would hang a little basket on the ceiling and things like that. So I hung clam baskets and this and that; anything people bring in or that I find really. We even went in the desert, near Lake Mead, and found an old boat, and I hung it in rooms five and six. A propeller, a turtle shell I took from Cecil Lynch. He used to have that turtle shell in his own restaurant, and it is still hanging in the bar at the Hole in the Wall now. Jimmy Durante brought a special basket that you put wine bottle and food in; it is still hanging down at the Hole in the Wall. Many of the Johnny Weissmuller memorabilia are there.

After six months or so we figured things out a bit and decided to drop breakfast and serve lunch and early dinner. A few months after that, as Mom was getting better to make dinner dishes, we switched to dinner only.

Rio in the Hole in the Wall kitchen

The kitchen at the Hole in the Wall in the 1970s

Also we changed the name of the Trattoria. *Butch Cassidy and the Sundance Kid* came out in 1969 and the name "The Hole in the Wall" kinda stuck in our minds, and I don't recall who finally said, we need to change the name of the restaurant to "Battista's Hole in the Wall"—maybe me or Rio—but it suited so we changed the name. I like cowboy movies, and the place was a little hole in the wall. So that is where the name came from. We didn't know we were going to expand like we did.

Word started to go around that I was singing pretty good: "There's an Italian tenor down there. Battista Locatelli." Many people came in for Rio's cooking and Battista's personality, the singing out front. Many chefs would come in as well. Of course, Rio was very attractive. I don't know if the chefs came in to help or to pat Mom's butt. Joke. That's a joke. Mom became quite the cook. She had a big following. She would be working in the kitchen, along with Pier and Desi, cooking at night and during the day, prepping the manicotti and lasagna and rollatini and this and that. Once Pier and Desi started having babies, they'd still go into the restaurant at five, six in the morning, and they'd strap the babies on their back and do the prep work: slicing mushrooms, cutting and dressing the garlic bread. Then they'd go home for a nap and be back in at night to serve dinner.

We had a sign, "Never on Sunday," but on Sundays we did have to go down and prepare the stuffing, make the chicken rollatini and other things. Lou Weiner, our lawyer, eventually convinced me to open on Sundays, too. That made things a bit more complicated as we had to hire additional staff and juggle a few more details with pay and scheduling.

Sergio Franchi headlined at many hotels in Las Vegas. He had a great, great voice. He would mention the Hole in the Wall when he was on stage. He was very impressed with our cuisine, and he would give us some suggestions as well. We became very good friends. On many occasions he would invite me to his show, and he would ask me up on stage with him to perform. He brought in many people to the Hole in the Wall over the years, like Ed Sullivan and his wife, Sylvia.

Hole in the Wall gang in the kitchen

With Sergio Franchi

Me with our chef, Georges Paire-Ficout

Rio and I worked hard

At one point I had a verbal agreement with Sergio Franchi to be my business partner. I needed seven more waiters and 10,000 dollars for a big expansion. The partnership thing never happened because he couldn't get license or this and that. At one point his manager, Trobner, said, "Don't invest any more money in that restaurant; it isn't going anywhere." So Sergio listened to his manager. He wasn't much of a manager because I paid Sergio back 250,000 for the 5 or 6,000 he lent me. That is the kind of person I am. Like I said, you give me the dime to make a phone call that means a lot to me—I don't forget that, I repay that.

We just kept growing and growing. Art Linkletter had a show called *People Are Funny*. And you know what? They do funny things. People, regular customers even, would dine and then steal our silverware. Why?

Eventually, we hired a chef who had a few ideas that we used. But hiring Georges Paire-Ficoult was one of the best decisions we made. He had been the chef at the Dunes. He came to the restaurant one day with some quail that this little Italian Mafioso guy that worked at the Dunes also was selling. George says to me, "Mr. Locatelli, I am selling these birds, and I think they would be great in your restaurant." Well, I told him, we don't even know how to cook these birds. One thing led to another, and George was in the kitchen as our chef.

Mom had a fit. She did not like the idea of being replaced, but we had such growing pains, we had to. We were very, very busy. Mom, Pier, and Desiree had to work like beasts. Everybody did. I could feel things falling apart a bit. Tempers were flaring between Mom and me. People were having to wait too long for their dinners because we couldn't get the dishes out fast enough; Mom was a perfectionist. So despite the good, the bad, the ugly, it was the best move to bring Georges Paire-Ficoult in. Later his wife, Paulette, came, too. Then came many, many others. We just grew and grew, and it became a real love affair, a real family place.

Rio went to work on the floor as a waitress for a little while after that. She and I were having some problems, some ups and downs. But we were bulletproof. We both hung there through the good, the bad, and the ugly, and

CHAPTER TEN

Rio and me with Dean and Gerda Koontz

thirty-five years later I sold the restaurant for multimillion dollars and everyone benefited from it. Are there things I would have done different with the Hole in the Wall? Maybe.

I made many friends through my years at the Hole in the Wall. Two of the best, best friends Rio and I ever made are Dean and Gerda Koontz. They were a young couple when they first started coming to the Hole in the Wall. Dean was one of our first customers and remained faithful through the years. Pier Leigh used to wait on them. When Dean and I met, he didn't have a pot to piss in, and I didn't have a window to throw it out. Now Dean's books are everywhere, and I've traveled enough of the world to see them everywhere for myself. One time when I was in France I saw a woman looking at Dean's books in a store. I told her, "I know him." She looked at me, paused, and said, "You're bullshitting me." Then I told her to look at the dedication page of *Whispers*. She saw the dedication and apologized when she saw the dedication to Rio and myself. Dean and Gerda always make their friends a priority, and whenever I have called, they have bent over backward to do me a favor, whether it is to send me a box of autographed books to give to some of our friends or have a little conversation. Every time he writes a book Dean always makes sure Rio and I and Pier get a copy. Looking back to when we first met in the early seventies, I realize we are going on almost half a century of friendship. That is incredible.

Every Saturday night, my family, including many of the employees, would walk to the Caesar's Palace after work. We'd get a matzo ball soup. We'd play keno. It was a good time. Even after working together all day, all week, we still enjoyed being together. It was truly a family restaurant.

Like most businesses, we had Christmas parties every year—sometimes at our home on Sloan or at the Hilton. But our best time was in the summer, around Memorial Day. We would go to the Warm Springs with the family and all of the employees. George and Paulette would organize the food and drinks. Vittorio would roast a pig sometimes. There would be games like soccer and races. It was really a laid-back, good time. As the restaurant grew, we started hiring buses to take everyone there and back.

There are a lot of memories of the Hole in the Wall. One time when I was working, the Spilotro brothers came in. You know, with the Mafia and all of that. They were kind of running things in Las Vegas at the time. So I called up Ralph Lamb and his assistant sheriff at the time, John Moran, and asked if I should be worried. They told me not to worry. "We already know they are in there. Our boys are in the restaurant undercover."

At one point the Spilotro brothers opened a pizza place and named it the Hole in the Wall. Lou Weiner called their lawyer, Oscar Goodman, who later was the mayor of Las Vegas, about the name of their restaurant and very easy, no problem, they said okay and changed the name of their restaurant. Considering who we were dealing with, I was a little concerned things could have gotten messy.

I remember one time getting a call from Sheriff Lamb telling me that a lady had called him to complain about the Hole in the Wall. She told Sheriff Lamb that our children were underage and serving alcohol. He told her, at least we knew where our children were and that things would be much better

The Hole in the Wall Gang in 1977

At a show at the Flamingo with the Weissmullers, our children, and some of our Hole in the Wall family and guests

if more parents knew what their children were up to. He told me not to worry about that woman if she complained again. After all these years, Ralph Lamb and I are still in touch.

Ralph Johnson and his wife, Faye Peterson, owned the Westward Ho. They were old-timers in Las Vegas and weekly patrons at the Hole in the Wall. Through that we became very good friends. For years, Rio and Faye, sometimes the four of us would meet at the Sands Hotel for breakfast and some conversation. I recall, Faye advised me on what to say before I met with the bank president, Horsey, at Home Savings because he owned the property across the street from the Hole in the Wall and I wanted to buy it.

When I went for my meeting with Horsey I only had five thousand dollars. I says, "I want to buy your property." "Okay," he says, "let's talk." So I tell him I'd like to buy it with five thousand down, and I will make a thirty-thousand-dollar payment every six months. I didn't even know how I was going to raise it. The Hole in the Wall had only been there a couple of years, and even though it was doing fairly well, I was putting most of the money back into the Hole in the Wall, buying out all these various leases in the shopping center so we could expand the restaurant. Horsey says, "No deal." I even told Horsey, "I will pay 7 percent interest on the money." Still he says, "No deal. Please leave, I am busy." Me, being persistent, I am the kind of guy, like a woodpecker, I keep pecking and pecking and pecking. Pretty soon he gets tired of hearing me. Who knows? Maybe that is how I made it happen. I left the room when he said no, but I came right back in and said, "Mr. Horsey, you are now the president of Home Savings. There was a time

With my daughter Heidi, around age 14

when someone opened a door for you. You want to sell this property, and you are not going to lose money; you will make money from me because if I don't pay, you've got five thousand in your pocket and every six months you've got thirty thousand, and if things go well with the Hole in the Wall, in no time you'll be paid. Just give me a break, please." He says, "Seven and a half percent and you've got a deal." I said okay, and I believe I had the property paid off in a year or so. In two or three years, I sold it for a phenomenal price. So that is what I did. I kept buying property here and there for investment. I have no recollection of losing money on any of the property I bought. Sometimes I invested with other people, like Don Romano. And of course, when I finally sold the Hole in the Wall to Harrah's—the reason they paid so much was location, location, location.

The union was big in Las Vegas and run by the Mafia. Al Bramlet had been in charge for years and was very powerful. I didn't want to join the union, but one day a union worker, Ted Dedesco (who later became a friend), comes in and says to me, "You'll have to join the union or you'll have problems." By problems he meant serious—life-and-death—problems. But the union dues were so high. He told me just to put my key people in it, like our chef and six or so others. He was a good man that I liked and that I had a lot of trust in. He came every month to the Hole in the Wall and went to my office and wrote his own check out. It was a good thing I joined the union, too. Things didn't go so well for restaurants that didn't join. Father-and-son hit men, Tom and Gramby Hanley, hired by Al Bramlet, used to bomb restaurants and cars. And of course you can look it up, when a bomb didn't go off, Bramlet wouldn't want to pay. One time he didn't pay and the Hanleys took him out to the desert and shot him. There is more to that story, but it was enough to assure me that Ted was right in telling me to join. Shortly after Al died, I was able to leave the union because the mobsters hold in Las Vegas and over the union was shaky, so I just had to pay a fine and I could be done with the union. Of course that fine was 137,000 dollars for not having all my employees in the union in the first place. I asked the union if I could just give that money to my workers instead and they said, "No way."

A man came in one day and said he was an accordion player and that he would work for tips only if I'd give him the opportunity. I was a bit skeptical; I didn't think we needed an accordion player, but I decided to give it a try. It turned out to be a big benefit to the Hole in the Wall. After a month or two, I ended up putting him on payroll and getting him insurance. Gordy has been with the Hole in the Wall for over thirty-five years now. People even mistook him for the owner on many occasions.

In order to expand our business, I started taking over the leases at the neighboring businesses in the strip mall. I bought the laundromat first in order to expand the kitchen in the 1980s. Bill Barnette came in and did the plumbing. We only shut down the restaurant one night. He revamped all of the pipes. Then Clark County Restaurant Supply helped us put together the new kitchen. Larry, the owner, saw we had excellent credit because we always paid our bills on time. Then we bought the beauty salon, cash checking, drugstore/barbershop. This is why we got so big; our office was all the way down

Employee and family photo at the Hole in the Wall in 1982

"Why don't you call it Pizza Rio?"

The Hole in the Wall in the 1980s with the MGM behind us before they moved.

to the jeweler. Within a year and a half the kitchen got huge. The roof was not made to carry that weight, so every time we took a wall out, we had to put a steel beam in. Along with Freddy, Richard Hall did a lot of work helping out with building the separate walls. Of course, Vittorio was there many, many times helping out.

We had this extra space next to the Hole in the Wall, and we decided to open a little pizza place there. Nanien said, "Why don't you call it Pizza Rio?" So that is what we did. At first Mom and Ellen and Joe ran it, but in later years we gave it to Gigli.

One year the temperature was up to 117, 120 degrees. The transformer on our power pole overheated and the power at the restaurant went out during business hours. We lit some candles and had small battery-operated lights going. Of course, we called the electric company right away and they said it would be four or five days before they could get to the transformer because they were so busy. Well, we had a customer, unknown to me, who was entertaining a group of people that night. "Battista, may I use your phone?" he asked. He made his phone call, and maybe fifteen minutes later a truck arrived and, within half an hour, I had a new transformer. It just so happened that our customer was the big CEO of Nevada Power. Oh, how sweet life is!

I had the first traffic light installed at Audrie and Flamingo. Before that there was only a light at Flamingo and Las Vegas Boulevard. I talked to the Flamingo, MGM, and Maxim Hotel. The Flamingo and Maxim each contributed 10,000 dollars, and I put in 27,000 dollars. The city covered the rest of the cost. It cost a total of 127,000 dollars in the late seventies when it was installed.

I met this man, John Salie, a veteran of World War II. He drove a cab—dropping off and picking up customers to the Hole in the Wall. We became friends. I invited him to come in the morning to the Hole in the Wall to have coffee and read the newspaper, and we would talk. It became a routine. I really enjoyed his company. One little detail about him—he was a real, real miser—oh, how he could stretch a penny. And sometimes he would ask if I needed anything done. So I asked if he could go to the bank and make my deposits from the night before. He'd take my pickup truck and that became a routine, and I would compensate him by treating him and his wife to dinner a few times a month.

Now it was about this time that I bought the shopping center from Joe Julian. I had already bought the land the restaurant was on from Al Levinson for 325,000 payable at 18,000 a year with no interest. The reason the land was so cheap was because Al Levinson had had a lease with Joe Julian for the land for years at 5,000 a year for ninety-nine years. I bought the shopping center from Joe Julian for 2 million, and I borrowed the money for that from Valley Bank. They lent me the money because I had good credit, and of course Lou Weiner was a great friend and our lawyer. He helped us to acquire the loan. My payments were to be 33,000 dollars a month. Business was booming at the Hole in the Wall, but the economy was rocky at this time. Jimmy Carter, the peanut man, was president. Overnight the interest went up to 21 percent. My payment with the bank did not change but my interest payment went up to 30,000 and only about 2,000 went to the principal. Meanwhile, I was supposed to have received the payment from selling the property across the street from the Hole in the Wall that I had initially purchased from Mr. Horsey at Home Saving. Behold! The Hotel Shenandoah who bought it from me went in Chapter 11. So my money was held up for a while. Therefore, I was getting behind on my payment to the bank, so when I was telling John Salie of my problem, he says to me, "Do you need some money?" So I tell him, "Yes, I could use 375,000 dollars as of yesterday." I had a cashier's check of 375,000 dollars the very next day. Just to show you the kind of people we were, there was no paper involved, not even did we shake hands—just our words. Of course I paid that money back with interest.

Now John knew I kept a gun in the backseat of my pickup truck. One day he took it and shot himself in the back alley of the restaurant. We were all so shocked. The police came and of course interviewed me. They asked me what I knew about him, whose gun was it, and what were my dealings with him. I told them it was my gun and that he had lent me 375,000 dollars. Of course, I said all of this not thinking that would give the police reason to believe I had motive to kill him myself. It was obvious that it was suicide, though. In fact there was a lady shaking out a rug from her second-story apartment window, not seventy-five feet away, who saw John put the gun to his head and pull the trigger. She screamed and at that same moment Pier Leigh was driving up in her car and saw him fall to the ground. I believe he had recently learned he had terminal cancer. The police took my gun for a couple of weeks and returned it, no problem. Can you imagine if this were to happen today? The news media would go crazy with this. When Lou Weiner called John's wife, who was Japanese, she said she wanted to go back to Japan but didn't have the money. She had no idea that John had lent me all that money. By this time, things had picked back up for me financially, and within two, three days we got the money to his wife and she was able to go back to Japan.

Chapter Eleven

Seeing Stars

Through the years anybody who was a somebody came into the Hole in the Wall. Hundreds of movie stars. Hundreds of entertainers. Many hotel owners. Jerry Lewis, Bill Cosby. One time, Bill Cosby and I took our shirts off and were showing off our muscles in the restaurant. Phyllis Diller, Ella Fitzgerald and her family, Wally Schirra—the man landed on the moon. Betty Grable; Noah Dietrich, Howard Hughes's right-hand man; and on and on. So many photographs. We could make a book just of all the photographs we have. We really made a legend of a restaurant.

My son Gigli actually played tennis with Bill Cosby about a dozen times, and I found out later, he cut classes sometimes to play. His school called me to tell me my son hadn't been there. I talked to Mr. Cosby about this and being the good man that he is, he called the principal of the school and vouched for Gigli and said something like, "You must understand how kids are." What kid wouldn't cut classes to play tennis with a celebrity like Bill Cosby?

We got some good publicity from Larry Glick. He was a news radio host back in Boston. He started calling me in the mid- to late seventies two or three times a week. He'd put me on the air and ask me about the celebrities that came in that night. I'd tell him Sheriff Lamb is here or Jerry Lewis or whoever and he'd ask to interview them. And they usually said yes because everyone knew who Larry Glick was. Then he'd have me sing a song. He called every week until I sold the restaurant. People would come into the Hole in the Wall and say, "Larry sent us."

We really got to know and be known by a lot of people in Las Vegas. The Hole in the Wall opened up some interesting doors and opportunities for Rio and me. In the late 1970s we were invited by the governor of Nevada and the mayor of Las Vegas to see Langley Air Force Base in Virginia. The Hole in the Wall paved the way for me to meet George Bush, Bill Clinton, and George W. Bush—three United States presidents. Not counting Richard Nixon and John F. Kennedy during my time in Hollywood. One time when I saw George W. Bush in Las Vegas, security would not let me near him to get an autograph, and I remember him saying, "Let the marathon man come through. Let the marathon man come through."

Johnny Weissmuller and his wife, Maria, would come into the Hole in the Wall once they moved to Las Vegas, and I never charged them any time they came in. He would sometimes do the Tarzan yell when he came in. Everyone loved it. We really became well acquainted. He became a host at Caesar's Palace. One time he broke his hip and someone painted his crutches like a zebra, and he gave me both of them before he passed away. I hung one up in the restaurant. I was given a few things of his when he died, like his Olympic watches. Rio and I cared a great deal for Johnny and Maria. When his widow, Maria, eventually died, we paid to have her body brought back to the States so she could be buried next to Johnny.

Betty Grable came into the restaurant a lot. I served her in Beverly Hills, but we didn't know each other then. But we got to know each other at the Hole in the Wall; she brought a lot of business to us. She brought in Alice Faye, Phil Harris, and many others.

One time Betty invited Rio and me to dinner. When she called to invite us she said she only knew how to cook one dish: corned beef and cabbage. I told her that it was one of Rio's favorites, which it is. Rio still recalls Betty's corned beef and cabbage was so good. While we were there I remember Rio and I went swimming while Betty sat by the pool with her legs stretched out.

Rio commented recently that Betty's legs looked every bit as good that day in her fifties as they did in her youth.

A day or two before Betty died on July 2, 1973, she called me. She had throat cancer, cancer of the lung, she was a chain smoker. When she called me, I didn't recognize her voice because it was so raspy, and it had been so clear. "Battista, this is Betty," she told me. And I says, "Hi, I didn't recognize your voice, Betty." She said, "You know, they've got me so doped up. I will be dying in a few days. I know, I feel it in my bones. Would you be kind enough to sing at my funeral?" She liked "On a Clear Day." I sang that for her so many times.

At her funeral I think I sang "On a Clear Day" and "The Lord's Prayer." There were many people at her funeral. Cesar Romero, Glenn Ford. Rio was sitting next to Hedy Lamarr and Mitzi Gaynor, and one of them said, "Oh boy, that man has a beautiful voice." And Rio said, "That's my husband." I did do a pretty good "On a Clear Day." I still have the telegram that Betty's ex-husband, Harry James, sent me after the funeral, thanking me. Betty Grable was a special lady. It truly was an honor to be asked to sing.

Ed Sullivan would come in to the Hole in the Wall. I already mentioned that Sergio Franchi first brought him into the restaurant. Once when Ed Sullivan came in with his wife, Sylvia, she ordered tea. She drank hot tea with milk. So I brought out her tea and a container of milk and set it on the table. She scoffed a little and Ed laughed a bit at that. What can I say? We didn't have a creamer. A little while later they surprised us with a little cow creamer as a gift. It is on our kitchen table right now as I record this.

Rio and I were invited by Sergio to have lunch with him and Liberace at Liberace's home one time. It was nice. Liberace was a patron of Battista's Hole in the Wall.

Once Robert Redford and Willie Nelson came into the Hole in the Wall together when they were filming *The Electric Horseman*. It was pretty funny because none of us knew who Willie Nelson was; he was a country artist. So everyone was giving Robert Redford lots of attention and ignoring Mr. Nelson. We finally figured it out, I think Pier realized it.

People like Andy Williams, Jimmy Dean (the sausage man), Robert Goulet, Florence Henderson, Connie Stevens, Jerry Vale, Sergio Franchi, Vikki Carr—they would invite our family to see their shows, and while we were there they would always ask me on stage, without any rehearsal, to perform two or three songs. It was a lot of fun.

At one point Jay Leno came into the Hole in the Wall. I wasn't there, but Doug Morgan was maître d' that night. Anyway, he talked about us on *The Tonight Show* shortly after he came in. That was pretty nice.

A typical evening at the Hole In the Wall with celebrities including Neil Simon, Rob and Carl Reiner, Ed Ames, Marsha Mason and others

With Slim Pickens and pals

Singing with Merv Griffin

CHAPTER ELEVEN

Michael Landon with his wife, daughter, and me

Ella Fitzgerald with her family, Rio and me

We always had a good laugh when Bill Cosby came in.

Clint Eastwood was also a patron. We even arm wrestled. Guess who won?

Luciano Pavoratti, Rio and me

With Guiseppe Di Stefano, the famous Italian tenor

Betty Grable and me

Telegram from Betty Grable's ex-husband, Harry James on my singing at her funeral

CHAPTER ELEVEN

Note from Ed Sullivan

Sylvia and Ed Sullivan with Rio and me

Farrah Fawcett has even dined at Battista's Hole in the Wall

Robert Redford group photo while excluded Willie Nelson looks on. Oops!

Johnny "Tarzan" Weissmuller, his wife Maria, daughter Lisa, his son-in-law, and me

Chapter Twelve

New Experiences
1980–2000

I went with Dean Peterson, co-owner of Westward Ho along with his sister Faye and her husband Ralph Johnson, to Anchorage, Alaska—we've had a lot of fun fishing over the years up in Alaska—with the Learjet and we talked about flying. Dean made the joke that I would never be a pilot because I had no education, my English, this and that. Well, I proved him wrong over and over, big time. August 10, 1976, I got my pilot's license and three, four months later I got my first plane. I eventually got four types of licenses, even seaplane landing for landing in and out of little lakes like Lake Mead.

Kathy Jones gave me my first lessons. I took a lot of lessons from Captain Colonel Robinson; he was the chief pilot for the Thunderbirds in 1962. He was a hell of a pilot. He later worked at the Hole in the Wall, and his daughter Linda was our head bartender and still works there today. I also took lessons from Bob Verhagen and Bob Fern.

Rio also got her license—maybe a year or two after I did. At the start, Kathy Jones suggested she get a crash course, in case something happened to me while I was flying and she needed to land the plane. But once she got started, even though she was hesitant, she was doing so well, she decided to get her license. So I surprised her with a Cherokee Archer airplane. I took her down to the hangar, and Ralph and Faye Peterson were there along with

CHAPTER TWELVE

My first airplane. A Centurion

Kathy Jones, and the plane was there with a big bow on it. Kathy says to her, "You might as well start your lessons in the plane you are going to be flying."

Since then, I've owned, bought, twenty different airplanes. Well, I kept the economy going there for a while. We can say that. As we speak now, I am coming up on my eighty-third birthday. Guess what? I'm still flying. It keeps me alert and my cells very sharp.

When the MGM burned down in 1980, I was out flying with Robbie shooting an approach (instrument-only landing, practicing under the hood) at McCarran. It was early in the morning, and we could see the smoke so we flew over before I landed, and for a moment I thought it was the Hole in the Wall. We could see people jumping out of the window of the hotel restaurant to safety and see the helicopter with ropes pulling people out.

25R at McCarran is the second-longest runway in the U.S. When they opened 25L, I believe in 1991, they wanted to run a 10K on it, so I sponsored the event. I had an airplane full of eight commissioners. I was the first person to land and take off on 25L. The liability was phenomenal. They really checked me out before they asked me to do this. Still today I am an icon at the Las Vegas airport. They have a lot of respect for me, and I have a lot of plaques to prove it.

When they extended and redid the runways, 1-9L and 1-9R, they called me again, and I baptized those. I was the first person to take off and land on them.

Once with Eddie and Patty Pardi we were flying to St. Thomas and went too far down to the next island that was not U.S. so we came back up and landed in St. Thomas. When we landed, they dissected the whole plane. They thought we made a stop down there to load some drugs and things.

On one trip to Acapulco with Lou Weiner and his wife, Judy, we were running out of gas so we stopped at a small airport in Mexico fifty or sixty miles before we entered the United States, but they were out of fuel also. Because I took Robbie as a copilot, we decided for him to take the Golden Eagle airplane alone to the border only to where there is a fuel station. The plane would use less gas since it was empty, and he made it with four and half gallons left, fueled up, and returned to get us.

I must mention that Lou was a great friend over the years. When he called the Hole in the Wall every morning at four-thirty or five in the morning, he'd say, "Good morning, you bum." Just a little memory. It is hard to find a better friend than Lou Weiner. Honesty was his motto. I was one of his pallbearers along with Harry Reid, Richard Bryant, and others when he died in February 1996. The funeral was at the Las Vegas High School Auditorium. Instead of a hearse to bring his casket, he had a Brinks money truck with a sign that said, "Sorry, ladies, I'm taking it with me." He was always a great jokester. We loved him very much.

An elementary school was named after him in 1990, and funny thing—the street running alongside the school is Battista Lane. Our friendship still continues.

I still enjoy flying today

Rio and I before a triathlon at Lake Mead

I did a lot of flying. Flew all over, day and night. Flew from Parowan to Las Vegas at two, three in the morning hundreds of times. Into Van Nuys Airport, which is one of the busiest general aviation airports in the world. Santa Barbara, you name it. Believe it or not I've had three nose-wheels give out on me. I survived all three incidents; two were in Parowan and one at McCarran.

In the early 1980s I went to Pritikin for the first time. Michael Gann, owner of the Barbary Coast, told me about it first. Rio and I went for one week the first time. It really changed my mind about some things. Each year after that first visit I started making changes to my lifestyle: exercise, diet, et cetera. All my life I already liked salad and greens, so it wasn't too shocking to me. But I have to take a moment to thank the people at Pritikin and say how grateful I am to the Pritikin program. I attribute my ability to go up fifteen thousand feet in my airplane without oxygen to them. I was able to run the New York

Marathon just three months and two days after my quadruple bypass surgery and that's why I am still physically and mentally strong today. Thank you.

It was Pier Leigh who got me started running. I'd get up every morning at two, three o'clock and go running—I still do. I'd meet with Marvin, Dr. Hoffman, Pier, Desiree, Sandy, and a few others and we'd run, then we'd meet at the truck stop and have a beautiful breakfast. How many marathons did I run? I really don't know. The first marathon I ran was with the mayor, Ron Laurie, of Las Vegas. I was in my fifties and my time was 4:04. I think I ran at least twelve marathons and many half marathons, many 10Ks, many 5Ks, many ten-milers. I ran until I was blue.

I ran the Boston Marathon three times—I even flew to Boston with my own plane to run the Boston Marathon. Desiree said four, maybe it was four. It was a lot of fun, lot of memories. The best time I ever had was in the Las Vegas Marathon, 3:16:47, and that was at sixty-six years of age.

My brother Mario also is someone who doesn't quit moving. Even now in his seventies he is still climbing mountains. He has climbed fifty of the highest mountains in the United States, he is the first seventy-year-old to climb Mount McKinley in Alaska, and even climbed Mount Kilimanjaro. He lives in Montana, and in the past I went hunting with my brother Mario a lot; with Horst Dziura, the president of the Flamingo; even Vittorio and my friend Ron Goreman. We'd meet Mario up in Montana and then we'd travel eight, ten hours into the mountains, sleep in a tent, rough it, and then go stand in the snow all day waiting for an elk. We did kill some animals, but nothing spectacular. Years later up here in Brian Head, Utah, Monroe County, I got some spectacular game. I killed one elk September the seventeenth, 2011. I think that is probably my last elk. Two of them I killed received the Boone and Crockett Club award and the club's presidential certificate because they had a certain length of the horn. The one I killed in 2006 I believe was 403. Big elk. So anyway, I enjoyed hunting. It was a challenge.

In 2001 we were planning a big, big party for our fiftieth anniversary. Unfortunately, I had some clogged arteries and had to have a quadruple bypass. Dr. Dadourian, Dr. Hoffman, Dr. Green—they really saved my life, and our friendships continue today. Dr. Nancy Donahoe was my surgeon, and four days after my open-heart surgery, I was out of the hospital. I missed our party, though. We didn't cancel it, as so many people were flying in for it. My family from Italy; my brothers and sisters, nieces and nephews even came; and my friends from Japan that I sang in *Madame Butterfly* with. So that was a disappointment.

After I was released from the hospital, complications set in. I was short of breath. Dr. Hoffman took me to the hospital since Dr. Dadourian was on vacation. From what I understand they found a lot of goop and blood left in me from the surgery. My heart wasn't free to pump efficiently. So I went back into surgery, and they sucked out all this buildup. I was in intensive care. They didn't know if I was going to make it; I was in deep shit. My legs and heart swelled up. Dr. Green came in and drained nine liters of water from my body. One of my lungs was deflated, so I was hooked up to a special machine to help my lung. I remember Rio came to visit and accidentally kicked over the machine and it broke! They didn't have another one for me to use. They should have put the machine in some kind of crate so that no one could accidentally do that.

It is a miracle that I am alive after what I went through. I was wired up like a robotic person, and after two or three weeks of being bedridden, I got up with my two little stands—you know, the ones that my wires and fluids are all attached to—and maybe I walked the length of a car. It took me maybe twenty minutes. I could barely walk. I was so weak, but I forced myself. The nurses told me not to. I told them to let me die my way, please. After I'd walk, I would sleep a couple hours maybe, and then I'd get up and walk. Two in the morning or ten at night. I wasn't bothering anyone, and I'd tell the nurses, please let me do this.

So I started to walk around, and each day I could go a little farther. I'd walk from one nurses' station to the next, and soon I only had one stand. They started taking out my tubes. Pretty soon I was walking a whole mile, and then I started to sing. I'd see people lying in their beds, in their rooms, and tell them, "Hey, you are gonna die in there. Get your ass out of bed and get moving." There were days I had five, six people walking with me. When I finally checked out of the hospital forty-one days after my second surgery, the general manager of the hospital gave me a letter that said, "It was an inspiration to have you here." He wrote that they lose a lot of people because they won't get up and move.

After the hospital I went to rehab and started to walk the treadmills, but I remember they didn't want my heart rate to get above 129 beats per minute. So they were constantly slowing me down. But prior to the operation I signed up for the New York marathon, and I was determined to make it there and I did.

On one of my 60 plus climbs up Angels Landing

Three months and two days after I left the hospital, I ran the New York Marathon. Dr. Hoffman went with me, as well as my daughter Pier and her husband, Randy. My time was 5:11.05. I came in thirty-sixth for my age division. Not too bad, not too bad. And today I can still kick my leg up six feet in the air, and I still walk a mile in less than fourteen minutes.

While writing these memoirs, I've been going up to Zion, to Angel's Landing. I've done that more than fifty times in a year and a half—from the age of eighty to eighty-two I did it fifty-five times. I'd do it more if it weren't for the drive and the winter weather.

Chapter Thirteen

The End of an Era

Through the years of having the Hole in the Wall, I have done it all: electrical, fix the roof, waiter. I was blessed with awesome common sense. There was nothing I could not do. Many times I had no choice. When the money started to come in, the business was getting so big, I had to concentrate on running the restaurant and hire people to do the fixing up and other various things to keep Battista's going.

The evening maître d' was eventually turned over to my son-in-law Jerry Pearson five nights a week, and then I only went in two nights a week. He was a great people person for the job. Some time in the 1990s I stopped completely. After Jerry and Heidi moved away, Vittorio took over for a time and later Doug Morgan permanently became our maître d'. At that point I just came in the morning to take care of the bank and paperwork and bills and check operations. But occasionally I'd still come in at night to sing and visit.

Speaking of Doug Morgan, I must acknowledge him for all his hard work. Other than maybe one year I recall, he has been with the restaurant since the beginning.

When we first opened the Hole in the Wall, there are five companies that I have to give five hundred thank-yous to: Bill Barnette (plumbing), Clark County Restaurant Supply, Dave Waugh and Virgil Weese of Robert's Electric, Lloyd's Refrigeration and sons, Hammond Sheet Metal and sons. We

Welcome to Battista's Hole in the Wall

had such growing pains; we kept growing and growing and these people never once asked, "How you going to pay for this?" They just say, "Pay when you can," and it worked out beautiful for me. I'd like to take this opportunity to say thank you a hundred times over.

Battista's Hole in the Wall was a very successful restaurant; it still is. Night after night—900, 800, 700 dinners. And we are only open from 5 p.m. until 11 p.m. That is a lot of dinners in six hours. One night Laura, when she worked the door, sat 1,038 people herself. Another night, when Vittorio was maître d', we did 1,092. And once when I was working the door, we did 1,093. Those were our three biggest nights. We have had people call in from Europe, Japan, all over the place to make a reservation at Battista's Hole in the Wall.

Over the years it has been wonderful to be able to give a job to family and friends. I was really happy to give a job to my nieces and sisters and brother and grandchildren. I must mention that Marcella was a wonderful sister to have work there—she really had our back over the years.

The Hilton Corporation, Barron Hilton, asked me a few times about selling the Hole in the Wall. One time I said, eight million. God, I'm glad they turned me down. Harrah's bought out the Hilton Corporation—they bought up many hotels in Las Vegas. It is the biggest hotel corporation in Las Vegas. Tony Santo, senior VP of Harrah's, asked me—"Hey, Battista, you still want to sell your restaurant?" I mention how much for and Harrah's said it was too steep. Shortly after that, another company called me and offered a million more. But I had told Santo he could have it first. So I told him that I was offered a million more with this other company, but I still gave it to Harrah's for the price I initially told them because I am a man of my word. In July 2005 everything was final with the sale of the restaurant.

Even since we sold the Hole in the Wall, it continues to be successful. Rio called my sister Marcella the other night, and she could not talk because

Battista's Hole in the Wall in the 2000s

they were so busy. Full house, every night. That says something. Why is it still popular? Because we have a good product with a warm atmosphere. The prices are still good to where people can come to eat and still go home with their wallet. All the wine you can drink, salad you can eat, bread you can eat—and it is good.

Perhaps the final chapter and most honored closing for me and my time as a restaurateur was being presented with the key to the city of Las Vegas. The mayor of the city, the honorable Carolyn Goodman, even proclaimed December 12, 2014 "Battista Locatelli Day." On the proclamation I received from the mayor, it says, "For his iconic restaurant which has provided locals  and tourists alike with an extraordinary Las Vegas experience for more than four decades." Although I no longer own the restaurant, it remains a legacy to my name, and it is mind-boggling that taking a chance on a "dive" could have led to so many incredible experiences.

We had a lot of great people who helped Battista's become the success it was. The whole family put together. It is a legend our family built. As of the end of 2014, it is still going strong at forty-four years. Mind-boggling. Totally unbelievable. Something to be so popular for so many years. We have much to be thankful, grateful for. It will go on for so many more years if they don't make changes. If it's not broken, don't fix it.

Afterword

Ciao

PRESENT

∽

God really was in our corner, I have to say. To go from a skinny little lad in Italy to where I am today—it is totally mind-boggling. I have a beautiful wife, family, all I could ever need. Plus. Plus. Plus. I have much to be thankful for.

I was a little rascal, a beast. Never slowed down to enjoy the fruit. I am learning now—a little too late. When you are eighty-two years old, you are at the end of your journey.

Guess what? This morning, the seventeenth of February at 5:30 a.m., I power walked two miles in twenty-six minutes and two seconds. The temperature was below freezing. That is my best time. Hahaha. I'm not going to die on a couch.

I'd like to end with this, my motto: Don't do tomorrow what you can do today.

Ciao,
Battista
☺